Notes / Ex

# One Dude's Guide to Being Bipolar

## How to Stay the Hell Out of Grippy Socks Jail, Achieve Anyways, and Abide Always

ARCH GRIEVE

Gem City Dudeist Priest LLC
Dayton, OH 45420

ISBN: 979-8-8692-6347-6

For information on ebook, audiobook, and video formats of this book, please visit www.gemcitydudeistpriest.com/bipolardudeguide.

Ordering Information:
Special discounts are available on quantity purchases by corporations, associations, conferences, non-profits, and others. For details, email gemcitydudeistpriest@gmail.com.

# Table of Contents

*To my future bride, Jay, who is my inspiration, my joy, and my peace.*

# Chapter 1

## Sometimes You Eat the Bear and Sometimes, Why the Bear, He Eats You

*Living with Bipolar Disorder*

It seems like these days everyone wants to say that they are bipolar. Or, they love to call other people "bipolar," when it seems like they are changing up their moods all of a sudden. What these self-deprecating labels and insults have in common is that they both fail to understand that everyone goes from one pole to another in various levels of extremity. That's just the range of human emotions and what we call "life." The issue for those of us who suffer from bipolar disorder is that we cycle through these moods largely independent from environmental factors, and we often ride these moods to their extremes of ending up in the hospital (on the mania end) or unaliving ourselves (on the depression side of things). We aren't just "moody," and sometimes you might not have a clue as to where we are on the spectrum. Hell, sometimes we don't have a clue where we are. More on that in chapter 10. If you picked up this book because you or someone you know suffers from bipolar disorder 1 or 2, congratulations. You're doing more to manage your care (or be there for a friend or loved one) than many people who suffer from this illness, and I think that's far out, dude.

I have been diagnosed on two separate occasions with bipolar 1, an illness characterized by very high highs and brutally low lows. They used to call it "manic depression," which I liked more, in part because it was at least descriptive. Bipolar tells you nothing about what you experience at those two poles of the spectrum, whereas being a "manic depressive" at least gives you a bit of a preview of what to expect.

Sorry, I mean "being someone who has manic depression." I mean, sorry, "being someone who has bipolar 1." There. That's what my therapist(s) would like for me to tell you. I've gone through quite a few of them in a relatively short period of time (more on that later), but almost all of them have told me that I'm not a bipolar *person*, I'm someone who *suffers from* bipolar disorder. It's an illness, they like to say, not who you are.

But I don't have any bipolar therapists either. It's hard to explain to someone who doesn't suffer from it just how all-encompassing the illness is and how it feels much more like *who you are* than it does *something you suffer from*. I remember one time telling my therapist that I couldn't tell if my indignant reaction to a group of friends of mine was justified or not, or if I was just overreacting, or if it was just because I was manic. Her response kind of shook me. "People who suffer from bipolar disorder always have trouble dealing with regular human emotions because your emotions are all over the spectrum so often and you can never trust yourself to tell for sure which of them are coming from the illness and which of them are just normal human emotions that everyone experiences." Oof. And they wonder why I just cut out the middleman and label myself "bipolar."

Now there are a lot of reasons why I would never let my therapist write a forward to this book, but chief among them is that they know what I actually do in real life. But my hope is not only that *you'll* take my advice here, but that *I'll* take my advice, as well. If absolutely nothing comes of this book, no one buys it, and it succeeds only in helping me remember what I should do when I'm manic or depressed, it will be very useful. If it helps anyone struggling with how to cope with a mental illness that causes many to go on disability, or roam the streets without a home, or even kill themselves, it will have been well worth it. If you buy it, that's just icing on the cake.

But going back to the whole "bipolar as an identity" thing, there's also always been something about wanting to separate the person from the illness that always struck me as a bit ableist. I remember eating lunch with a friend of mine who had a son who suffered from "the disease," and knew how "the disease" I suffered from "warped my mind." And he was very nice and all and I learned a lot from him, but I also heard loud and clear (and not just from him, but from every therapist I've ever had and nearly all my non-bipolar friends) that it's definitely an abnormal condition that is not to be celebrated. It's something to be ashamed of, hidden away, or (at most) acknowledged as an affliction. But never valued or appreciated.

And that's true in spite of the fact that there are tons of famous bipolar people who have shaped our world (both for good and for evil, obviously, but I digress), and had an outsized impact on their time and place. Many of them continue to do so. And whether you want to or not, you will hear from us. And we will change your world. Sometimes we'll make it better, but that's certainly not always the case. And we may need to be dragged kicking and screaming to a care provider when you try to get us the help we need, but we'll probably love you harder than the other people in your lives do, too. But man, if you try and "fuck us in the ass" or even just step "over the line," then we're coming for you (or at least angrily shouting at you to "shut the fuck up, Donny").

Just ask fellow bipolar person Buzz Aldrin. He may have been one of only a dozen people ever to see our world from the vantage point of the moon, but you pick a fight with him in a random Hollywood hotel under false pretenses and he'll punch you right in the fucking face. But what would the world be without a single Carrie Fisher movie, or a Selena Gomez song, or a Kurt Vonnegut, Jr. novel? It would be a slightly shittier one, at the very least. Admittedly, I can do without the politics of fellow bipolars like Winston Churchill or Alexander Hamilton… they weren't exactly occupying various administration buildings in college, and they certainly weren't original authors of the Port Huron Statement. But you can't deny their impact on the world we live in today, even if it wasn't 100% positive. Plus, to many Brits and Broadway fans, Churchill and Hamilton are heroes. Of course, that's just, like, their opinion, man.

But I'm sorry, you *are* going to get a Mel Gibson or a Kanye every once in a while who just refuse to take their meds. Then again, if Kanye spends more time with his therapist than with Alex Jones, maybe he'll put out another *808s & Heartbreak*. But many of us understand the importance of taking our medication in order to provide stability in our lives, and who don't just drink whiskey every morning for breakfast (like a certain former British Prime Minister). "Everything in moderation" is key. Including the unhealthy stuff.

Truth be told, I haven't even been living with bipolar disorder for that long. Well, that is to say, I haven't exactly accepted my diagnosis until relatively recently. My initial diagnosis happened way back in 2012, after an incredibly stressful and prolonged work situation, which I believed at the time was the only thing responsible for landing me in the hospital. For weeks, though, I was going on 2-3 hours of sleep (at best) per night while essentially trying to act as a union rep for a school with no union, and doing all of this as a second-year social studies teacher.

The new principal of the school I taught at was, in short, probably a sociopath. Probably the only one I've ever met in real life. And as a person who suffers from another mental illness, I can't hate the guy, but I also recognized that he was willing to destroy the school that my colleagues and I loved and had collectively built into the special thing that it was for the sake of salvaging his own personal reputation. In other words, he had stepped over the line, and that aggression just would not stand, man. So we got rid of him. A dear friend of mine and I helped spearhead the effort to bring forward multiple student and staff complaints to a (very selectively) hard-of-hearing school board in order to try and ensure the safety of our students and teachers. During that time, however, I slept incredibly little, and tried to manage being a second-year teacher who was also running a student-staffed school store and sitting on multiple committees. I don't know when I would have had time to sleep (even if I wasn't also trying to lead a coup d'état). There was simply no time.

One day, though, in addition to the sleepiness, I started imagining things. I wrote strange emails to people because, in hindsight, I was paranoid and delusional; both symptoms of mania for me whenever I become manic (as I now know). Eventually, one night I was sitting at home, completely delusional, and just sort of, you know, getting a bit "out there." Not merely "out of it," but fully thinking-that-the-FBI-and-Chinese-government-were-both-after-me-for-some-reason-and-that-I-was-an-international-spy kind of delusional. That night my ex-wife and ex-sister-in-law didn't know what was wrong, but they knew I needed sleep. So, they gave me a sleeping pill, which I chased down with a beer. Then, instead of going to sleep, I proceeded to stay up and watch TV while they sat on the couch trying to figure out what to do for me, (and don't worry, there will be a whole chapter on drugs later on…).

Shortly thereafter, as I listened to the FBI helicopters surround my house, I was whisked off to a safehouse somewhere in the Greater Dayton, OH area. Well, actually, it was simply decided that I needed to go to the hospital. That FBI stuff, it turns out, was all in my head. As was the radio report I thought I was listening to about our "escape" on our way to the "safehouse." I don't know what they told me to get me into the car to go to the hospital, but I do know that on the way there I thought that the radio was broadcasting the story about our escape from Chinese detention (it was an NPR-style reporter, in case you're wondering how real the hallucinations are) and actively reporting on our journey to the safehouse that I was convinced we were traveling to, OJ-Simpson-in-a-white-Bronco style. Needless to say, I was confused when we arrived at the hospital. Convinced by my ex and (then) sister-in-law that I was in need of psychiatric help, I checked myself into the hospital. To this day I can't remember what my reason was, but I was then put on a hold and shipped off to a psych unit miles away from the hospital, where I spent one of the most traumatic weeks of my life. In hindsight, perhaps it was at the point where I put a (thankfully clean) bedpan on my head (for reasons I can no longer remember) that finally led them to conclude that a hospital stay was necessary. But who can tell?

The problem with being delusional/psychotic/having hallucinations is that everything seems so real. To this day I still can't separate all of the facts from the fictions that my brain made up. What I do remember, however, was desperately trying to get out. I eventually figured out how to get an attorney and fought for my release and won, but it was a bit of a Pyrrhic victory.

You see, they had put me on a ton of medications. I'm talking to the point where I was higher than a rocket man throughout the day. But I wanted to get back to work as fast as I could (I was a bit of a hopeless workaholic at the time, which Dudeism has saved me from, but more on that later, as well). So, I told my psychiatrist to get me off all the meds as quickly as possible, which ended up taking months to do safely.

I found it somewhat ironic that my psych at the time explained to me that there was a 50/50 chance that I was, in fact, bipolar. Turns out I was so bipolar that even my diagnosis was bipolar. But, I led a normal life for another seven years or so. I quickly got back into teaching and excelled—so much so that I was honored by Ohio's Council for the Social Studies with the Emerging Educator Award (bestowed upon new teachers who "show great promise" and "excel in their field"). And later that year, I went on to enroll in a dual master's program for international and comparative politics and public administration. I only finished one of them, but I did still finish it, and was honored with the Outstanding Student Award (presented by the college of liberal arts) *and* the Outstanding Graduate Student Award (presented by the graduate school at the university I was attending). I also ran for and won a seat on my hometown's local school board, and then went on to be the vice president of one local non-profit and the chair of another. I even switched careers entirely (twice!) and worked as a community outreach director, and then later became an internationally-certified transformative mediator. In short, I did a lot.

All of that came crashing down, however, when I was hospitalized for a second time. This time I didn't have all of the stressors in my life to blame for what I had come to describe as a "stress-induced episode of psychosis," like I did when I went into the psych ward the first time. Life was pretty good, and my job wasn't really all that stressful, yet my mania still ramped way up and I stopped sleeping and became extremely paranoid and delusional, all of which went on for a while until I finally checked myself into the hospital once again. But more on all of that later, too. The point is that I could no longer deny that I was, in fact, suffering from some kind of illness.

Since then, many of the things in my life that I thought were just character flaws and/or quirks have made much more sense now that I understand them to be symptoms of bipolar 1, and I have gone back and forth from mania to depression more times than I care to count. But, at least now I have a diagnosis, more education about my illness, meds, a better support system, and a much better understanding of what works and what doesn't work for me in dealing with it all. And that's what I hope to help you find in this book, as well. Being diagnosed as bipolar can be scary, especially when you don't know much about the illness. If you've just received a diagnosis, my goal is to help you understand it more and prepare you for some of the challenges you're likely to face. I'll point out some common pitfalls that I and others have suffered from, while also demonstrating that you can not only survive such a diagnosis – you can actually thrive in it.

As a secondary goal, I also hope that this book is helpful for any readers who have friends, family members, or lovers who suffer from bipolar. You're not my primary audience, but I do hope that having a better understanding of the disorder will help you help others in your life who, at times, may not always be able to help themselves. At the very least, I hope it gives you a bit more patience in your dealings with them.

Also, some of my readers may know me from my TikTok channel, where I go by my alter ego, the "Gem City Dudeist Priest." Dudeism is a bit of a joke religion that started as an homage to the movie *The Big Lebowski*, and while nothing about the religion is serious, it *has* seriously helped me cope not only with the illness, but with life in general. So, you'll have to forgive all of *The Big Lebowski* references sprinkled in (or, in some cases, dumped liberally) throughout the book. Does the religion help me? Absolutely. Do I want you to become a Dudeist? I honestly couldn't care less. And that's sort of the point. Part of the reason I love it so much (particularly as an ex-evangelical) is that I don't have to proselytize, so I truly don't give a fuck whether you join or not. But if you do, welcome to the rug, dude. Oh, and everyone is a dude in Dudeism... "dudette" is just not the preferred nomenclature. Just dude, in the parlance of our times, please.

*Our emotional support cats, Dude and Bunny (both are female felines who identify as dudes).*

But what *is* Dudeism, you might ask? Well, it's essentially a religion based on the cult classic Coen Brothers film, *The Big Lebowski*, and there are hundreds of thousands of adherents all over the world takin' her easy for all us sinners. At its root, the religion is about abiding through all of the strikes and gutters the world throws our way, and learning how to be at peace even when Nihilists are trying to steal your joy. Practically, that looks like smoking a lot of weed and drinking a lot of White Russians. But just like all religions, we have our holidays (like Dudesmas and The Day of the Dude, to name just a couple). And say what you will about the tenets of international Dudeism, at least it's an ethos. Some people like to say that it draws not only from movie quotes, but also from Taoism. I haven't found it to be Taoism, exactly, but as religion knockoffs go, I find that it stands up on its own pretty well.

*I take my religion very seriously, dudes.*

With all of that out of the way, let's start with one of the more exciting aspects of having bipolar disorder: experiencing mania. Strippers and blow await you in the next chapter, so if you still prefer to jerk off manually, then grab the lube and let's dive in.

# Chapter 2

## I'm Sorry Your Stepmom is a Nympho

*Dealing with Mania*

It's hard to know where to start with talking about mania. So, let's just start with the exciting stuff: let me tell you the stripper(s) story. Of course, they say that the brain is the biggest erogenous zone (at least for some people, anyways), so I'll do my best to paint you a story even wilder than that *Logjammin'* flick you love so much.

For a little background, by the summer of 2022, I had been married for many years (17, to be exact), and things weren't exactly going as well as, say, Maude and Jeffrey. My "Cynthia" (aka my ex) at the time didn't even want me to help her conceive, man. And, to quote my favorite show of all time here, "not that there's anything wrong with that." But the rationale given, which was that she didn't want to have a bipolar kid, did bother me perhaps a bit more than I let on. I still remember the first time I told someone and they said, "wow, that's a little shitty." To which I replied, "I mean, maybe… but at least I don't have to have kids." And at the time, I didn't *want* kids. Until I met my one, true special lady friend: Jay. Now I'm looking forward to having some Little Lebowskis on the way some day.

Now, if you just don't want to contribute more to global warming and the constant and devastating depletion of the earth's natural resources more than you already have by creating a mini Achiever of your own (especially when there are already so many other young children of promise out there), then I would say kudos to you, dude. But the other reason (not wanting to bring another *bipolar* Achiever into the world) *is* a little shitty, I'd now have to agree.

But I decided I needed to take a trip to Bosnia to buy myself a vacation home one month in 2022 while I was hypomanic. In hindsight, I can say that perhaps I was even a tiny bit manic. I even remember making a TikTok video at the time that was pretty self-aware, noting that I probably *was* making impulsive decisions due to the mania. But I told myself that it was under control. My personal spending habits, however, told another tale.

*Me at the Sarajevo Film Festival with Nastasija and Pavle.*

I basically bought a ticket to Sarajevo and stayed in Bosnia and Herzegovina for a month and a half. During that time, I was doing a lot of things… as one does when they're manic. What people don't understand about being manic is that you feel like the entire universe is connected and everything is on a single wavelength. Sometimes you get feelings of grandeur and start to think you're the only one who can see that wavelength and operate within that space. It can lead to a confidence that is unmatched, which means you tend to be more outgoing. Personally, I was using that confidence to get places I normally wouldn't exactly be invited to otherwise. I was meeting and interviewing popular artists (such as the turbo-folk sensation from Bosnia and Herzegovina, Fazlija, who got even more popular thanks to his TikTok hit, "Helikopter Helikopter," and Dji Dji Jankelić, the so-called "Bonham of the Balkans," who introduced the double-bass pedal to the former Yugoslavia) and interviewing them on my podcasts. I was meeting with politicians (such as Benjamina Karić, the Mayor of Sarajevo), and Serbian television and movie stars (such as Belgrade journalist Nastasija Stošić and her boyfriend, the TV star Pavle Mensur, who were really nice when talking with me at the Sarajevo film festival, which I got into with press credentials thanks to my local Discover Dayton podcast). All of that was well and good and it was a blast meeting those people.

*Me with Fazlija, the turbo-folk sensation who dominated TikTok for a while with his hit song "Helikopter Helikopter."*

I also happened to be mulling over my decision to get a divorce during this time. I remember thinking through it and writing down my rationale. I also texted a friend to see if she would talk with me about my decision and help confirm that I wasn't making it simply due to mania. I still remember where I was during that conversation. I had actually hopped on a plane and flown to Serbia for a day because the first time I had come into Bosnia and Herzegovina, I hadn't gotten some stupid form stamped, and the easiest way to do that was just leave the country and come back. So I went to Belgrade that night and played poker at one of the only casinos I could find that had live Texas Hold 'Em. After winning enough money to cover the cost of my ticket, I talked with my friend for a long time in that casino, debating whether the decision I was making was simply because I was manic, or was actually the right call. In hindsight, the mania definitely played a role in deciding, but in this instance, it was definitely the right call. This is something I've also noticed about mania… oftentimes you become a different person while you're manic, but sometimes, it simply accelerates the things you were already going to eventually do. Or it can make you more willing to share things that you've always been thinking, but have never been willing to speak up about beforehand. I walked away from that conversation determined to go through with getting a divorce, a decision I can truly say I do not regret in the slightest.

As an aside, I think there's a tendency many have to view a marriage that ends in divorce as a failure. I don't. I learned a lot during those years, and I'm grateful for the good times we had together. There are certainly many things that being married kept me from doing that I would have liked to have done, but that doesn't mean I regret it. When it comes to marriage, shit just happens, man. Plus, as someone who is (now) in an age-gap relationship, dating my fiancée at the age I was when I got married would have landed me in prison. There's no point though in worrying about what happened in the past, because it will never change. I still think (sometimes) that it's worth worrying about the future, but really the only time you can do anything about it, anyways, is in the present. So that's where I like to stay, whenever possible.

But don't misunderstand; I'm not someone who gave up easily on my marriage. We had both been to individual therapists to work through things, and we tried couples' therapy multiple times. We always reached the same outcome, however: she was upset with my adherence to a strict drug regimen, while I felt that she was just too uptight, dude. And if you haven't guessed already, Dudeism is kind of all about not being so uptight. I finally decided that I had traumatized "that poor woman" enough and that things likely weren't changing, so I reconciled myself with the fact that our marriage had run its course.

The shitty part, now, (and where I start to become an asshole in this story), is when I tell people that your sex drive increases exponentially when you're manic. Meanwhile, I'm a guy living in a foreign country who is becoming increasingly manic and whose libido is going up every day. But I also didn't dare tell her I wanted a divorce, because (I believed, although later found out it wasn't true) that she had a power of attorney and the ability to lock me up in the psych ward again, which I really didn't want to happen. And so, rationalizing my actions by telling myself that telling my friend (but not my wife) that I intended to get a divorce was sufficient, I started going to Sarajevo's sole strip club, where I became a known regular. I would walk in and they would start pouring my usual rum and coke (White Russians weren't on the menu) and ushering me over to the women I could ask to go with me for a trip upstairs.

Now, I never did the math, because I didn't want to know. But I reckon I easily spent upwards of $10,000 over the course of a month and a half on strippers. And I won't lie... I didn't have a bad time. Plus, in my mind, I was saving money. Not at all dissimilar to "girl math," as it's known on TikTok, "bipolar math" is a real thing. Basically, it boils down to having a mindset when you're manic that convinces you that you have unlimited cash reserves and all purchases are warranted. But I also recognized that a US psych ward stay was around $10K, as well, so if I was going to spend that much money one way or another, I might as well have some fun, right?

The problem was that I *did*, in fact, have (practically speaking) unlimited cash reserves when you consider that I was bumming around in a lesser-travelled Eastern European country that had a very favorable exchange rate with the US. As a result, it felt like I was flush with cash, which I thought (at the time) would never run out. And it didn't... not there, at least. In addition to consuming large amounts of alcohol, I was also going to hookah bars all the time, smoking a lot of weed (I counted 6 drug dealers I managed to meet during my short trip... that's a new one each week), plus a little cocaine. LSD was readily available to me, as well, I just didn't think it was a good idea. Unfortunately, I couldn't find my favorite drug: mushrooms. So it goes.

But, all good things must come to an end, and I had to get back home to return to teaching in Dayton before the fall semester started. Once there, I would begin the long and arduous dissolution process. While I was over in Bosnia and Herzegovina, I was able to tell myself that I wasn't cheating because I was just "looking," and I would soon be ending my marriage, anyways. I also rationalized my behavior by telling myself that I still likely saved money on strippers vs. paying for a hospital stay, and it was immensely more fun. I still felt guilty, however, and I timed my return so that I would get back home and then have to leave immediately to go to a podcast conference I had been planning to attend in Dallas, Texas. I'm also an internationally-certified transformative mediator, but I can tell you from experience (including that of my own) that mediators are world-class conflict avoiders, and I'm no different in that regard. So, I left for the conference without seeing her.

*One of the highlights was getting to meet "the Bonham of the Balkans," Dragan "Dji Dji" Jankelić. He is a super nice guy who let me interview him on my podcast, Discover Dayton.*

Once I got there, it was a great time and super helpful for my own podcasting venture (which is why it's such a bummer that I stopped doing both of my shows for about a year pretty much right after the conference, of course... but they're back now, finally). While I was attending the conference I was going to the sessions during the day, interviewing people during the afternoons, and then would go out afterwards for dinner. I even made a friend from the UK who I enjoyed hanging out with regularly. One night, however, I got the itch to go to a strip club again... they're addictive, after all. I googled nearby clubs, found one that looked pretty promising, and called myself a Lyft. Now I won't go into the details of that night, but I do remember later discovering that my hotel was next to the JFK assassination site and thinking how it was funny that I could now say that Lee Harvey Oswald wasn't the only one who got some head in Dallas. Terrible joke, I know. But after that night, I really had nothing left to hang my hat on with regard to the whole "not cheating" lie that I had been telling myself. The truth was, of course, I had begun cheating well before my Dallas visit. I had cheated in Sarajevo, Belgrade, Chicago, Dallas, and Dayton, too.

This all begs the question, I suppose, of why I'm sharing this openly in a book about bipolar disorder. And I guess for me, at least, the most important reason is that I want to help you understand just how easily you can start to rationalize your shitty behavior when you're manic in a way that could ultimately come back to haunt you. Or, it could simply be at odds with how you want to show up in the world. There's a Vonnegut quote from *Mother Knight* I love, that goes, "we are what we pretend to be, so we must be careful about what we pretend to be."

The simple truth is that I was pretending to be an unmarried man before I was one. More importantly, I was pretending to be one before I had told the person I had pledged to be faithful to for the rest of our lives that I was leaving the marriage, and that's the part that's fucked up and that I would never do to someone again. So, I guess I share the story as a warning to let you know that you can do some pretty out-of-character things when you're manic, so you have to be very careful. Which is why I called my friend first to make sure I was doing the right thing with getting the divorce in the first place. And thankfully, it was definitely the right call, because I'm so much happier today with Jay than I ever was in my first marriage, and I can't wait to be married to the right person this time.

But, of course, manic people do rationalize a lot of things, so here's how I rationalized my behavior to myself. For starters, I was manic, I was ending my marriage, and I had a legitimate reason for not wanting to tell my ex I was leaving the marriage but also didn't feel particularly bound by its rules anymore. Mostly that meant that I didn't want her to use my behavior (of seeking a divorce or cheating) as an excuse for deciding to have me committed. Was I still an asshole for it? Absolutely.

Was I likely wrong that this was possible for her to do? In hindsight, probably. Would I do that to anyone else ever again? No, definitely not. But, do I regret the experience *outside of* the whole "cheating" and "spending large sums of money" aspect? Not at all, no. Also, for legal reasons, the thing about the blow jobs was just a joke.

*Lounging in an inner tube at Lazy Bar in Blagaj, BiH, quite possibly the most dudely bar I've ever been to.*

You see, young Arch grew up in a sexually repressed conservative evangelical household, so up to that point, I had had sex with exactly one person: my ex-wife. So, it was definitely somewhat liberating, and the only moral problem I feel guilt about is that I did all of it behind her back (and wasted so much money on myself). Otherwise, I am of the opinion that strippers provide a very valuable service in keeping lonely men (and women, and people of all gender identities, really) from feeling so alone, and I think that's something to admire. Hell, I've even dabbled in a little selling of tasteful nudes of myself here and there. Being in the smut industry is work. *Logjammin'* is work. Sex work is work. I just prefer a union shop, is all.

What else does it feel like to be manic? It's hard to explain, but "hyper-energized" probably gets the closest for me. You just want to *DO*. You don't care so much *what* (or *who*) you do, you just want to do it (or them). Right away. *Now.* And that is hard to sustain. You get very little sleep, though, so you're kind of exhausted all the time, but you also have a lot of reserve energy. You forget to eat because you're just doing, and your brain is moving at a breakneck speed. Everything, and I mean *everything*, is just a connection waiting to be made to something else. Maybe it's two friends you want to hook up, or two ideas that are very disparate that you somehow find a way to connect, or one fact that you start to couple up with a delusion you have. You want to make all of the connections, and you feel like all the world is one. It's a kind of high, for sure.

Another thing that can happen (if things get really bad) is that you can hallucinate, which is kind of scary. I have a number of hallucination stories I could share, but my fiancée has a favorite out of all the ones I tell. It's the time I thought my friend, Aaron, was a cat. Don't ask me how (or why) he became a cat. He just did. And I was sitting in my backyard talking with him while my ex and my mom tried to figure out where the fuck to take me for my second hospitalization. My bipolar story chest is full of little treasures like that one.

You also become very trusting when you're manic, which is odd because (I, at least) also get very paranoid. But for me (and I've learned that I'm not alone in this), everyone becomes either friend or foe. I trust the "friends" implicitly… often far too much. There was the time I "bought" a car from someone who was "selling" their vehicle on Facebook marketplace. I showed up and checked it out, it looked good, so I gave him my info, put half down for it, and was going to have him deliver it to my place. Once the check cleared, the dude disappeared. Multiple calls and texts led to the inescapable conclusion that I had been duped… and I was out about $1,500. So it goes. I'll find you though, David. And I may or may not have found your last place of residence on one of my manic "brother seamus" sleuthing missions. I'm closing in! Again, for legal reasons, I kid.

There was another time before that too, in Bosnia, where I bought a Yugo when I thought I was going to be moving there for good. But I couldn't legally own it yet, so I put it in a friend's name. When I decided I wasn't going to be living there, I simply gifted it to her. Legally speaking, of course, she already owned it, so it was the easiest thing to do. But damn, there goes another car (two in one year) that I essentially paid for and then gave away. Well, maybe you can't "give" away something you never had, but that's neither here nor there. I was sad to see the Yugo go, though. It was a glorious beacon of Yugoslav-communist manufacturing, and I loved it very much. I will always miss it. But you usually can't hold onto all your manic purchases. More on that in a future chapter.

So how do I deal with it all? Well, I keep my mind limber with a strict drug regimen, of course. But a lot of it is listening to those around you and listening to them when they say they are starting to see signs of mania, because often you're the last one to know. Unless you're really good at masking, and then sometimes you can fool everyone *and* yourself! There was one time like that when I was sitting in my office while my ex went and told my boss how I needed to go to the hospital. They actually kicked her out and thought she was the crazy one... even going as far as banning her from my workplace! I checked myself into a hospital later that afternoon, hallucinating and no longer able to register what was real and what was not. The delusions can hit hard, for sure. But I still managed to fool all of my coworkers into thinking I was fine that morning, and that's how mania works.

How else do you know you're manic? You get racing thoughts, your speech speeds way up, you start spending lots of money, you see connections everywhere, and you get a lot of shit done. That last reason is why shows that glorify the worst elements of bipolar (cough cough *Homeland* cough cough) make it seem like manic bipolar people are super productive and should go off their meds to tap into their creativity. In all honesty, the creativity piece remains intact, I've found, and staying on your meds enables you to actually keep up with your ideas and follow through on some of them. So *don't* go off your meds. I know the struggle is real and all, but just don't. More on that later, too.

My advice for making it through mania? Work with a therapist and psychiatrist to get your mania under control. They make drugs for it now. I have a cocktail that works pretty well for me and hopefully you can find one that works well for you. But also get someone close to you who you will allow to speak into your life when you're doing too much or throwing your money away and give them the permission to do so. Make sure to warn them that you might not want to listen, however.

And if, by chance, you're someone reading this who is a friend or loved one of someone with bipolar... first of all: thank you. It's hard being friends with us, I know. One coping strategy I've developed over the years is accumulating a lot of friends (although many are really just acquaintances), so that when I do become manic and inevitably need a favor, (whether it's picking me up from a bar I had no business being at in the first place, or just listening to my crazy-ass rants), I won't lean on any of them too much. Which is not to say I haven't done that. Some of those people have stuck around and they're real ones for sure. Others fade away. And that's OK. I get it. I don't know if *I* could always handle me at my worst, either.

Secondly, you might want some good advice for helping your friend or family member or significant other through a manic episode. The first (and arguably most important) is this: don't take anything we say too seriously. And we may say some mean, awful, horrible shit... and it might even be directed towards you. Some of it may have some basis in reality, but for the most part we are unable to control our thoughts or emotions and may even be delusional or hallucinating (or both), so take everything we say and douse it with the biggest salt shaker you can find. If we have big plans, talk through those with us. Don't minimize them or say it's not possible, but ask us practical questions to help bring us down to earth.

Whatever you do, though, *don't lie to us*. Because we'll probably find out, and then we can't trust you anymore. More importantly, we're trying to separate out fact from fiction in our brains, and our brains are already lying to us, so we don't need someone else doing the same thing and making us further question what's real or not. Don't argue or debate with us, though, that's usually not very helpful. Asking leading questions that leave breadcrumbs for us to get back to reality, though? Priceless.

Another simple thing you can do is encourage us to eat and drink. The easier the meal is to prepare, the better. And if we're really far gone, you may have to prepare it for us. But often we simply forget to eat, and that doesn't help anything. Pair that with a lack of sleep and the clock on us being checked into a psych ward starts ticking faster, like you just cut the wrong wire on a time bomb. Sleep is absolutely critical to bipolar people all of the time, but that's especially true when we're manic. Our physiology is such that while manic, we don't think we need as much sleep and we have a ton of energy and too many ideas to sleep on, literally. We can't stop working on our projects or fixating on some issue that we can't get over. Ask almost any psychiatrist and they will tell you that sleep is the best medicine for any bipolar person, period.

And when we're not sleeping, a quiet and non-stimulating environment is best. Whenever you can get us to chill in front of the TV for a while and do nothing, another bipolar angel up in heaven gets the gift of mood stability. But finally, don't leave us alone. And it's also a good idea to get us to turn off our phones. Avoid letting us hang out with people who tend to feed off of and encourage our impulsive behaviors and, whatever you do, don't let us make large financial decisions. But more on that later.

Next up, let's take a look at the flipside of the bipolar spectrum of moods: depression.

# Chapter 3

## These Men are Nihilists, Donny

*Dealing with Depression*

So one thing to understand about bipolar depression is that it's more episodic than unipolar depression. That is to say that there is usually a much clearer beginning and end to bipolar depression, and often the depression will come right on the heels of a manic episode. It might seem cruel that a disease that can cause you to spend your way into massive debt without a second thought while manically chasing your dreams can then give you debilitating depression right as you realize your ambitious plans won't pan out. And that's because it is. So it goes.

But, the fact that it *is* somewhat predictable actually helps, in my opinion. I can sometimes remind myself that the depression will go away eventually, like it always does. Sometimes when I'm at my worst and I can remind myself of this fact, my brain actually believes me enough to let me complete a simple task like taking a shower. Which I guess is a good time to talk about symptoms of bipolar depression, which are largely similar to those of unipolar depression.

Obviously, the side effects that everyone associates with depression are present: you get sad and anxious. Depression often goes further, however, and makes you feel worthless and like nothing really matters. In short, you become a Nihilist. And like those Nihilists, you might even resort to cutting off a toe, or (more likely) hurting yourself some other way. When it gets really bad, you might even think about (or commit) suicide.

Let's talk about that for a minute, though, because I don't think a lot of people are fully aware of the alarming statistics. On average, bipolar people die younger. That's because, according to Psych Central, bipolar disorder has the highest rate of suicide among all mental health disorders.[1] In fact, we commit suicide at a rate that's about 10 to 30 times higher than the average population.[2] It's even worse if you consider just men. But out of all bipolar people, well over half of us have attempted suicide, and NAMI believes that up to 19% of us are successful.[3] So it goes.

But let's say you don't experience the worst of the worst. Life can still suck, don't worry. Often depression will cause you to become slow or lethargic (which, without the depression, isn't all that bad), or cause difficulty sleeping. You may not want to eat now, so you lose weight. Your speech slows way down, if you even have anything to say at all. That reminds me, one of the most annoying things you can tell someone with depression is "you seem quiet." We know we're being quiet. You're lucky we're even listening to the conversation, because we also have difficulty concentrating, and if we manage to listen and concentrate enough to follow the conversation and then articulate a thought, just know that it took incredible effort. We often don't want to do anything or go anywhere, and we start to care very little about a lot of things. Nihilism at its finest, perhaps. It's when we become hopeless and start to feel worthless that the suicidal thoughts really begin to rear their ugly heads.

So how can you help us? Well, obviously, if we're suicidal, then don't leave us alone (and if we like things like guns and knives, see if we'll let you take those and keep them safe and away from us until we're feeling more ourselves). In fact, if you can help us develop a suicide safety plan before we need it, you'll be even more amazing. See the appendix for an example. But if we're lonely, just be there with us. You don't have to say anything, because we probably won't want to. We're often very happy just to listen to someone else talk, so read to us or turn on a movie and just be present. Sex doesn't hurt, either. You know, coitus.

But you don't have to come over and "fix the cable," of course. In addition to a little logjammin', showing an interest in trying out some of our hobbies can be one of the best ways to help. The last time I got

<hr>

[1] "Do People With Bipolar Disorder Think More Often About Suicide?", Hope Gillette, February 16, 2022, https://psychcentral.com/bipolar/suicide-in-bipolar-disorder.
[2] Ibid.
[3] "Bipolar Depression: The Lows We Don't Talk About Enough," Katherine Ponte, September 22, 2021, https://www.nami.org/Blogs/NAMI-Blog/September-2021/Bipolar-Depression-The-Lows-We-Don-t-Talk-About-Enough.

out of the hospital I started doing pottery. Am I a good potter? Not at all. Did I find it therapeutic to make something out of a literal lump of clay? Absolutely. My fianceé recognized how much it helped and now we have an old kiln and make pottery together sometimes. It's one of the myriad of reasons she's such a keeper. But one of my favorite Kurt Vonnegut quotes of all time is his advice on taking up the arts. He said, "The arts are not a way to make a living. They are a very human way of making life more bearable. Practicing an art, no matter how well or badly, is a way to make your soul grow, for heaven's sake. Sing in the shower. Dance to the radio. Tell stories. Write a poem to a friend, even a lousy poem. Do it as well as you possibly can. You will get an enormous reward. You will have created something."[4] I couldn't say it better myself.

But what can you do for yourself? Coax yourself into working on those passion projects you have. Read that book. Or write that book. Or watch that movie you've been meaning to see. Binge-watch the entire catalogue of *Ink Master* in all its 199-episode glory. Whatever it is, *just do it*, in the parlance of our times. Also, if that thing you do happens to be physical, such as yoga or Brazilian jiu-jitsu, that's even better. Staying active truly does help you mentally. And even though you'll never want to go, you know you'll always feel better after you do.

So what about those times when you're manic *and* depressed at the same time? You know, being bipolar, you might think it would be nice to be right in the middle of those two extremes sometimes. Of course, there's two ways to find that compromise position: you can be in a state of euthymia (balanced mood), or you can have a mixed episode (which combines the worst, sharpest edges of the double-edged sword that is bipolar disorder).

A mixed episode is when you are, indeed, both manic and depressed at the same time. Never is someone more of a true manic/depressive than during a mixed episode. One minute you might think you've found the cure to solving world hunger, and the next you don't think you can do your job well enough anymore to go into work. It's its own special brand of shit sandwich. A good day to you, sir? No, I think not.

---

[4] Kurt Vonnegut, Jr., A Man Without A Country, (New York: Random House Trade Paperbacks), 24.

*You want a toe? I'll get you a toe. A ceramic one, that is. You don't have to be good at pottery to do it!*

But, if you want to watch what happens when you fuck a stranger in the ass, Larry, then do something to slightly piss off a manic/depressive. One minute they may want to verbally annihilate you into oblivion, while the next they may question whether they should even exist (you know, given how pointless life is and all). The best thing you can do is be there and be a non-judgmental friend who *really* (and I do mean *really*) doesn't take things too personally. Eventually we'll stop being assholes, though, I promise.

Now that we've looked at the highs, lows, and everywhere in between, let's turn next to something that can help alter your mood for the better (or for the worse): your drug regimen.

# Chapter 4

## Keeping Your Mind Limber

*Drugs, Alcohol, and Bipolar Disorder*

Comedian (and living testament to the fact that you can be an incredibly successful bipolar person) Taylor Tomlinson talks openly about suffering from bipolar disorder in her stand-up (and, as an aside, she's really great live). In one of her sets, however, she has joked about how being friends with bipolar people is like being friends with someone who can't swim. It's like "being friends with a normal person, except there are some places you just can't go." But, as she likes to say, "they make floaties" now. That's what drugs are: your floaties.

As I write this chapter, I'm running on a strict drug regimen designed to keep my mind limber (and functioning). Allow me, if you will, to give you a quick breakdown of each drug I frequently consume and explain whether or not I find it helpful in dealing with my bipolar. And when I say every drug, I mean *all* of them, starting with caffeine. Any of these alone and/or together may or may not be helpful to you, but they work for me. Some of them, anyways. And, of course, I have to preface all of this by saying that this is just one dude's opinion on what works *for him*. See a doctor, though, when making decisions about what drugs to use when limbering up *your* mind. Preferably one who's a good psychiatrist, (and thorough).

Let's start with caffeine. Caffeine by itself won't necessarily tend to be terrible for you in small amounts, but if you're manic (or prone to it) then you should probably limit your intake to no more than three iced lattes a day, as caffeine can help trigger mania.[5] And while we're at it, smoking isn't great for bipolar either. It's been found to be associated with mixed episodes, manic cycling, and more severe episodes… so,

---

[5] "Is it safe for people with bipolar disorder to consume caffeine?", Morgan Meissner, June 7, 2022, https://www.medicalnewstoday.com/articles/bipolar-disorder-and-caffeine.

not great.[6] That said, nearly all of the people I know who are bipolar smoke one thing or another. But we also do a lot of things that aren't great for us. "All things in moderation" is a key tenet here. Chain smoking during your manic episodes isn't great (says I, as I chain smoke my way through the White Owl sweets I bought this morning – "do as I say, not as I do" applies here, dude). While briefly dabbling in the process of smoking cessation, I learned that you can even smoke *tea*! What a time to be alive. Well, apparently they were smoking tea in China millenia ago. Must be some kind of an Eastern thing, I guess. I just learned about it recently, though. It's just OK as a substitute, although I have to say that at least it's much cheaper than tobacco.

And let's round out things that aren't great for bipolar people by discussing alcohol. I have a tricky relationship with it, as do many bipolar folks. Before being diagnosed, I was already a heavy drinker. That didn't really slow down at all after I had my first hospitalization. And honestly, it didn't slow down until I met my new special lady friend (aka my fiancée), who has helped me cut back a significant amount. I would suggest, however, that when you become manic or depressed you cut it out entirely. Allow me to illustrate this with a story.

One night around Thanksgiving in 2022, I was still dating my new special lady friend (or SLF), Jay. She was busy that evening, so I went out to one of my favorite bars in Dayton, Toxic Brew Company. They have a great house-made beer selection and some high-ABV beers (I love the Belgians they have, but 9%+ is kind of steep, even for me). Well, one thing to know about being manic is that it increases your proclivity to experiment with all drugs while *also* increasing your appetite for them, as well. So of course I got absolutely trashed. I was wise enough to know I needed an alternative way home, but I wasn't "all there" otherwise. So I called another Jay, my best friend from high school, to come get me. And come he did. Get me he did not. He decided to wait out in the car and text me that he was there, but I didn't hear it. By the time I realized he was there 45 minutes later, he had already left. I was livid. I started cussing him out over text out accusing him of abandoning me. In reality, it was my fault. Blaming others for your behavior is

---

[6] Elena Estrada et al., "Nicotine dependence and psychosis in Bipolar disorder and Schizoaffective disorder, Bipolar Type," *American Journal of Medical Genetics* 171, no.4 (2016): 521-524.

something bipolar people tend to do when manic, so friends and family: consider yourselves warned.

Having lost my ride option, I decided to order a Lyft home. Only problem was I was living in a camper at the time that was almost 40 minutes from that bar. So, after spending around $50 on a Lyft, I arrived home completely wasted, and crashed. Little did I realize that I had let my phone die, so my SLF was worried sick about me all night since I wasn't responding. To make matters worse, my propane had run out, so I was stuck in the cold camper with my kitties curled up in a bunch of blankets with the space heater going all night.

I woke up and realized I had fucked up and that SLF Jay was probably worried sick, so I walked across the street to a restaurant, phone and charger in hand, to try and siphon off some electricity. It didn't work. At one point I even tried to use a little hand-crank operated charger to awaken my phone long enough to send a single text message. I hadn't gotten an arm workout like that since I took too much Viagra one time, but I also didn't get a charge. So, I went to the people who I was trying to purchase the property from (which is a whole other story for another chapter… but I digress) and asked them to charge my phone. Once it was charged enough to power on, a slew of messages popped up from my SLF (and friends) asking if I was OK. Eventually, they were asking me if I was alive or not. Suffice it to say, I had reached the point of having a drinking problem and realized something needed to change.

As a result of all of this, I cut out alcohol completely for a while and then (gradually) reintroduced it. Cutting out alcohol entirely was something I hadn't done in over a decade, and it was sorely needed. I had developed a heavy drinking habit… I could go to a night of trivia and have a pitcher of beer and (maybe) leave feeling slightly buzzed. Now, that much alcohol in such a short amount of time will make me throw up, which I learned the hard way. Figuring out whether you're capable of having a relationship with alcohol or not, though, is something every bipolar person should do. Or at least that's, you know, just like, my opinion, man. And I say having a relationship (vs. having a healthy one) because alcohol isn't really good for anyone, but especially not bipolar people. Unfortunately, bipolar people also tend to have higher rates of alcoholism.[7] This is understandable given that it's an (albeit unhealthy) way to relieve anxiety and forget about your problems. But it's not a good one. I'll suggest a better one later on in the chapter (cough cough *weed* cough cough). But, it often works (temporarily), and that's why so many of us abuse it. At the end of the day, however, it can help increase the likelihood of going manic or becoming depressed, and make symptoms of each worse.[8] Sometimes you can't recover from it, as depression and alcohol usage can be a deadly combination, unfortunately.

My suggestion is that, if you're going to drink alcohol, at least cut back on (or cut alcohol out entirely) when you're manic or depressed. And even when you're *not* manic or depressed, you should probably cut back on alcohol. If you find yourself drinking more than two drinks per day or binge drinking frequently, you're probably drinking too much, dude. Slow it down a bit.

Now, I know that seems like advice you wouldn't hear from a Dudeist, but don't worry, I still abide with the occasional White Russian (although my favorite drink is actually an Old Fashioned), and I tend to mostly drink socially these days. All that being said, we can't cut our vices out entirely, right? Weed is my drug of choice when it comes to my own strict drug regimen that I use to keep my mind limber and abiding. And yes, many doctors will tell you it's not good for bipolar people to use weed. And I hear them, I really do. But at the end of the day you're the expert on how your body works, so listen to it. I've listened to mine and, on balance, I find that doing a J is more helpful than it is harmful for me. Let me explain why.

Research conducted in the past decade has shown that cannabis usage amongst bipolar people can, in fact, have a positive impact.[9] One study in 2015 found that cannabis usage by bipolar folks can enhance their mood.[10] I would have to concur with this. And it's not just when I'm

---

[7] Susan Sonne and Kathleen Brady, "Bipolar Disorder and Alcoholism," *Alcohol Research and Health* 26, no.2 (2008): 103-108.

[8] "Bipolar disorder and alcoholism: Are they related?" Simon Kung, February 13, 2024, https://www.mayoclinic.org/diseases-conditions/bipolar-disorder/expert-answers/bipolar-disorder/faq-20057890.

[9] "Treating Bipolar Disorder with Marijuana: Is It Safe?", Traci Angel, November 18, 2019, https://www.healthline.com/health/bipolar-disorder/marijuana-and-bipolar.

[10] Ibid.

depressed. I've found that anxiety and paranoia tend to accompany my manic episodes, and (for me, at least), cannabis helps with both symptoms. It can even out my mood as well, and it allows the racing thoughts to subside for a while when I medicate during particularly intense mania. But it's not just on the manic side. I've found that cannabis can help my depression as well, as it helps lift my mood, increase my appetite, and reduce my anxiety… all things that are typical challenges for when I'm depressed.

In fact, those same researchers found that even though these things *do* help people suffering from a manic or depressive episode, bipolar people tend *not* to use them during the times that they would be most helpful.[11] So, if anything, you should probably be consuming more weed, not less. But hey, I'm not a doctor, so this is not medical advice. If you want that, listen to Episode 97 of my Killing Time With Arch Podcast, where I asked Dr. Mary Clifton, (@marycliftonMD on TikTok) how weed affects people with bipolar disorder.[12] I'm just telling you what works well for me (and, anecdotally, a lot of my bipolar friends).

Another (possibly less talked about) reason to medicate with weed would be that it helps reduce your alcohol intake. At least, for me, it does. What I've found is that when I'm consuming cannabis, it makes me thirsty (obviously I'm not the first to discover this downside to the green stuff… cotton mouth is real, my friends). But as a result, I tend to drink things like water or other hydrating liquids when I'm smoking (instead of alcohol, which dehydrates the body). And if you compare the two (whether it be for bipolar people or the "normies"), alcohol is far worse and has much more potential devastating effects than weed does. So no, I don't mind if you do a J while being bipolar, dude. But if it doesn't help you, don't do it. Simple as that.

Which brings up a good point: the same drug cocktail that works well for one person may not help someone else at all. In fact, it could make them worse. I have such stories to share. Starting with Abilify. This drug was prescribed to me after I got out of the hospital for the second time, and at first I thought it was working. It's a mood stabilizer, and it

---

[11] Ibid.

[12] Arch Grieve, host. "Killing Time Episode 97 – Interview With Dr. Clifton," *Killing Time With Arch*, podcast audio, December 2023, https://open.spotify.com/episode/5YW9FPQrnuXDgo6cpespgn?si=cab62fcd5d2a4a8d.

was trying to do just that. To some extent it succeeded, as my mood was pretty stable while I was on the medication. Unfortunately, it was a stable depression. That's right. I was depressed. For like a year. All because of this stupid pill. I shouldn't say stupid, though, because I know many people have had success with it. For me, though, it caused insomnia, depression, anxiety, and more. It wasn't worth it, so I tried a different drug regimen (with the help of my psychiatrist). He switched me over to lithium, which I had dreaded trying because taking it often requires regular blood testing, and I hate having my blood taken. I don't mind shots or things going *into* my body, but I hate it when things go *out of* my body, particularly through a syringe. But now I'm currently taking that twice a day, Wellbutrin once per day, and Olanzapine, an anti-psychotic, as needed. I take that when I get particularly manic (like enough to where other people start to notice), and it helps me slow down the racing thoughts. It makes me shake more, though, than the lithium does, which is annoying. But it's worth it.

Now, finding that combo that works for me has taken a long time. I've tried a lot of different options over the years. Some I tried for a year or more before switching. Others I tried for just one night. I've also been on other mood stabilizers, like Depakote, and anti-psychotics, such as Risperdal and Latuda. Latuda gave me the shakes (or tardive dyskinesia, to use the preferred nomenclature). It was too much for me, so I stopped it after one night. Lithium doesn't seem to make me shake nearly as bad, so it's manageable. I also take Wellbutrin, which is an antidepressant. It's controversial to prescribe antidepressants because they can trigger mania. But, many doctors do it. Isn't it funny that they think taking a pill that might increase your mania is worth the risk, but smoking a plant that does the same (but also has beneficial side effects) *isn't?* Makes you wonder if Big Pharma is influencing our doctors... but I digress. I choose to take pills *and* plants, and both work for me in different ways. So if you're getting frustrated that one drug combo isn't working, just remember there's always another combo to try, and eventually you'll figure out that balance of side effects and positive benefits that's worth putting up with. Just don't go off your meds and go all Kanye on us... No one likes a bipolar person off their meds. Not even you.

*White Russians and weed are obviously important sacraments in Dudeism, but when you're manic or depressed be sure to be mindful about how much you consume of both.*

Also, you'll see a lot of meds that say they shouldn't be taken with alcohol. Often that's because it enhances the effects of alcohol (i.e. makes you sleepier or more aggressive, etc.). That's one reason a lot of people don't take their meds, which I think is a bad idea. That being said, "you've gotta live your life," as one pharmacist told me when I asked him if I could take a particular drug with alcohol or not. Plus, you're a cheaper date. But he did something I find very valuable, which is that he listed the side effects and then left it to me to make a decision. That's how I wish doctors treated us all the time. Because at the end of the day, as I like to say, all medications are self-medications (as long as you're taking them by choice). This is true because ultimately, I have to decide that the medication is worth taking, and the doctor's job is to convince me why it will help and educate me on the pros and cons of taking it so I can make an informed decision. That's how I think it should work, at least. So be honest with your doctor. And if you don't feel like you can, you really need to find another doctor. But at the end of the day, whether you have bipolar or not, you're literally poisoning your body (albeit with delicious liquids) when you consume alcohol, so let's not pretend there's a truly "healthy" way to drink, and finally stop judging bipolar people who choose to consume alcohol or weed or anything else they choose to put in their bodies, particularly if it's not harming you. End of rant.

And I would be remiss if I didn't mention that non-alcoholic beers and even spirits have truly stepped up their game recently, so I'd definitely check those out during your manic and depressive episodes. You can find a lot of decent NA beer alternatives, if that's your thing, but you can also find a lot of non-alcoholic spirits. In Dayton, there's a coffee shop I like to frequent called "Ghostlight" that sells NA spirits, and they really are capable of making some delicious cocktails. I would argue that the ones out there trying to replace other spirits (like whiskey or rum alternatives) aren't nearly as good as ones that are just trying to make interesting flavors. I've found a really good mix of some to make an excellent Negroni substitute, for instance. It's no White Russian, of course, but it's a nice substitute when you need to cut back.

Now that we've covered some of the many ways in which you can keep your mind limber and abiding, let's talk about maintaining your friendships next.

# Chapter 5

## Shut the Fuck Up, Donny

*Friendships and Bipolar Disorder*

*Keeping friends as a bipolar person can be challenging, but the real ones will stick around.*

Remember that story from the last chapter about how I asked a friend to show up and take me home from Toxic Beer Company in Dayton when I was hammered? That's my buddy Jay. Jay has been friends with me since high school. We've been through a lot together, including getting arrested on Christmas Eve one time. Thankfully, we found Xenia's version of (fellow Ohioan) Ron Kuby to make sure the fascists didn't throw him in the slammer for too long.

But say what you will about Jay, and you could say a lot of things about him; at least he shows up when you need him. Sure, maybe he doesn't always have the best ideas when I'm manic, perhaps, but he definitely is a ride-or-die friend who will always be there for you. Keeping these kinds of friends in your life as a bipolar person isn't always easy. Sometimes being friends with a bipolar person can end in a breakup. If you have a bipolar friend and you're reading this, you're already an amazing one. Doing your best to understand the illness and how it impacts your friend goes a long way with us, dude, thank you. So what does being a good friend to someone with bipolar look like? Let's dive into another story to discuss.

*How many friends buy portraits of you from your ex and display their collection proudly on the wall of their dining room? As far as I know, Jay is the only one!*

As I write this, I've just ended a relationship with my poker group (which I belonged to for over six years) and I just participated in a meditation with four former friends to discuss their decision to remove me from a board we served on together. How do I get into situations like this? Well, there could be many reasons, but the bipolar certainly doesn't help. If I had to explain what happens from a 30,000-foot view, I would say that going manic can cause us to make poor decisions that often put unique strains on our relationships with our friends. Let's take the example of my poker buddies to illustrate what I mean.

Last year, as I was planning to move to Bosnia, I decided that I had to let my poker buddies know that I was leaving. They expressed some sadness and then quickly moved on to finding my replacement. As bipolar people often do, however, I changed my plans. Like I've mentioned, I met someone, fell in love, and decided not to leave. I said as much to my friends via group chat, but the response wasn't what I had hoped. I didn't hear people say, "we're glad you're staying," and with my paranoia, I quickly started to worry that my spot had already been filled. A poorly worded text from a friend solidified in my mind the idea that I wasn't being invited back, and as a result, I lost it. I left the group chat and let my friend know I hoped that they liked my replacement. Not my finest hour.

It took a lot of reassurance from my friends to let me know they wanted me around for me to feel OK again, but one of my biggest fears is being abandoned. And I don't think I'm unique in that regard amongst bipolar people, either. Being a good friend to a bipolar person includes making sure they don't feel that way.

Now unfortunately, the story doesn't end there. It actually ends almost a year later. In between those events, my "friend" who hosted the poker club every month had been asking the group members to pitch in and get a new table. I thought our table that we used was just fine, so I constantly pushed back. Others did, too, but I was probably the most vocal. After backing down on the idea of purchasing a $1,000 table, he decided that we should buy a new $600 chair set instead, even going so far as to purchase it first and ask us to reimburse him later. I pushed back once again, but I happened to be somewhat manic, and ended up doing so in a way that was, in hindsight, somewhat confrontational. He wasn't having it this time, and he got defensive and lashed out at me. Admittedly, it's a stupid argument that we both blew out of proportion. But as a mediator I can tell you that it's almost never about "the chairs," or whatever else the argument is about on the surface. It's almost always about the decisions behind the actions we take that actually tend to upset us the most.

If you don't have a bipolar friend, you may not know this, but we can be downright assholes when we're manic. So I let him have it. One toxic thing I do when I'm manic is I'll attack all your greatest insecurities if I think you've really wronged me. I hate that I do it. It's not me. But it also *is* me… when I'm manic, at least. As of this writing, we haven't recovered from that, and I'm no longer in the poker league. So it goes.

This is why, however, I try not to get into arguments with friends (or loved ones, or anyone really, for that matter) when I'm manic. When you're manic, you're much more irritable and prone to anger. You're also not as good at critical thinking or self-censorship. Many times, you say things that you might believe are true, but come out wrong. In other words, you may not be wrong, Walter, you're just a manic asshole. So hold off on sending that manifesto-length email to your boss, or calling your mom and dad and telling them all of the ways in which they have wronged you over the years (at least until you can calm down a little). Maybe you can say it differently to avoid ending a relationship. Maybe you don't even need to say anything at all. Just be cautious, dude.

But honestly, I'm OK with how my relationship with the poker "friend" ended. I don't really regret what I said to him. And maybe I should. But at the end of the day, I don't need friends who are actively hostile towards me when I'm manic. And, as they say, if you can't handle me at my worst then you don't deserve me at my best. I wish I could spin it differently, but if you're bipolar, be prepared to lose some friends. It's going to happen. And if you want to keep them in your life, you're probably going to have to get good at apologizing, so either learn how to do that well, or learn how to make new friends, or learn to be happy with fewer of them, because it's an unfortunate reality of living with the illness.

One way that I like to cope with being bipolar is telling people about it. I tell almost everyone, in fact. I even put it online and talk about it with my TikTok audience. I've also done storytelling events where I've shared about it, and I always tell my students that I'm bipolar. Why do I do such a scary thing, you ask? Because it helps destigmatize the illness. Some folks are truly terrified of bipolar people. There's so much misunderstanding and even more misconceptions about what the illness is and how it works out there that you'll have to forgive your family and friends for not being able to always separate fact from fiction sometimes. If they're actively trying to learn, that's great. Encourage it. Because we need more understanding people in this world, period.

Another reason I'm open about my diagnosis is that whole stigma thing. I can't tell you how many students and friends I've had over the years who have expressed thanks to me for talking openly about my disorder, because it helps them feel empowered and realize that they're not alone in having a brain that works differently. It also helps them recognize that they can be successful in managing it, as well. And I'm not saying that I'm always a shining example of what excellent self-managed care looks like 24/7/365. But I do have a pretty good handle on it now, and even when I didn't, I still talked about it, because the more we normalize talking about mental health illnesses, the less fear we have of them. We are fearful of what we don't understand, so the solution is more education. The more we educate ourselves and others, the more understanding we all become of one another. At least, that's my theory of how talking about it works.

But you should be prepared for some things to happen when you're open about your diagnosis. One unfortunate reality is that people will often dismiss things you say or feel, and blame it on your bipolar disorder. It might be an idea you have that they reject out of hand. Or, maybe it's a concern you have about their behavior towards you that they claim is warranted because of your mania or depression. Whatever they choose to blame on your disorder, it doesn't really matter. Don't ever let them use it as an excuse to humiliate you or treat you disrespectfully. You're not just bipolar *sometimes*. You're bipolar all of the time. Your mood is going to fluctuate, and they're going to have to learn how to deal with that. If they want to dismiss an idea you have or a concern you bring up because of your bipolar, ask them if it's OK to wait and talk about it at a later time when they feel (or you feel) you are in a better frame of mind. If they refuse to do this, I would recommend you hold off on discussing it further until you are both ready to discuss it after you're in a better place. If they can't handle that, then that's on them. But do be prepared for lots of excuses for others' behaviors to be blamed on you and how they think you might possibly react. It's fucking annoying, but it's a reality you'll likely experience forever.

Another thing you should be prepared to do is to help your friends out, too. Be there when they need someone to complain to about their spouse or job. Show up when they have that moving party because they can't afford movers. Bring along a ringer suitcase full of your dirty undies when your friend has to make a drop to help free a young trophy wife who has (possibly) been kidnapped. Just be as good of a friend as you possibly can, and the good ones will stick around and help you when you need it most, as well. What hurts more than the possibility of losing friends, though, is losing your significant other. So, let's talk about that next.

# Chapter 6

## She's my Fucking Lady Friend

*Romantic Relationships for Bipolar People*

So, you found that special lady friend, did you? Or guy? Or enby? Whatever their preferred nomenclature is, it doesn't really matter. Here's what I want you to take away from this chapter: it's difficult, but worth it, to be in a romantic relationship with someone who is bipolar. Additionally, for my bipolar folks who are reading this, I want to give you some tips and tricks on how to be a little less burdensome to your partner (or partners... this is 2024, after all) during your manic highs and depressive lows. Now here's a brief history of my love life bona fides for you.

*The special lady fiancée and I in Spain on a rooftop bar in Barcelona in 2023. She's my best friend and the most amazing partner a bipolar guy could ever hope to have. She's also fucking hot.*

As mentioned in a previous chapter, I grew up a bit of a prude. That didn't mean I didn't like the ladies, however. I went just about as far as my brainwashed (and conservative, Evangelically Christian) conscience would allow me to go without believing I would be cast forever into the fiery pit of Hell the next day. Practically speaking, this meant a lot of making out and some (mostly) over-the-clothes stuff. No coitus. Looking back, perhaps it was a good thing, because as I write this at age 37, many of my high school friends are now celebrating the graduations of their first-borns. And not that there's anything wrong with that. It's just not for me.

I honestly can't imagine having spent my 20s and early 30s with a kid. I would always tell people that I'm too selfish to be a parent, and (as a teacher) didn't like the idea of taking "work" home with me. And that's what I recognize raising kids to be: work. These days, they don't even provide you with any economic value whatsoever (they're a huge net loss), and there's no guarantee of them caring for you in our old age. My parents are still under the delusion that their bipolar maniac of a son will be the one to rely upon when they're entering their sunset years. But then we all have to tell ourselves little lies, I guess. The truth is that now that I'm in my second marriage-bound relationship, I *do* want kids. A little Lebowski on the way, if you will. I'll say that it is understandable that my ex-wife didn't want them though, because (in her defense)… I'm already a lot. I was a lot worse when I didn't believe I had it, and before I got on a strict drug regimen, too. Regardless, though, she didn't sign up to marry a bipolar person. It wasn't until after ending a 17-year marriage that I found the woman who actually wanted to (knowingly) marry a bipolar person… and even have kids with them, no less! If my ex-wife was a good caretaker, this woman is a saint.

And I say she's a saint because I didn't have my life figured out when I met her. Quite the opposite, in fact. There's an old saying that you don't date on potential, but if she *was* sizing me up, I would have had very little to offer. I was a former high-performing individual who (in my mind) was past his prime and planning to move to Bosnia and Herzegovina to live out his days in drunken excess and debauchery (on the cheap, of course… I'm lazy and of Scottish descent, after all). Once we were together, however, I felt like much more was possible again. I started dreaming again about a future with her that didn't amount to pure escapism. I got my drinking under control… save for a night here and there where I forgot how much my tolerance levels had lowered. In short, I started trying again.

So some people ask why I got divorced. And to be fair, I technically didn't, I got a dissolution. I digress… but I guess I would say that if the relationship you're in doesn't serve your purposes anymore and neither of you is happy and you've given it your best shot, it's probably not worth it to continue. You get one life here and it's too short to spend it with someone who doesn't make you happy (and vice-versa). And thankfully I've found that person. It's an age-gap relationship of 11 years, for those who are wondering. As an aside, one thing I've noticed about age-gap relationships is that every couple who is in one thinks that *their* age gap is acceptable, if not perhaps stretching the limits a bit. None of them think they're too far apart, though. If yours is higher, however, they always think *you* are. But whatever. That's just like, their opinion, man.

And that brings me to my first piece of advice, which is to not get married when you're young. Maybe you want the kids, but (and unless there's a good reason for it) you'll have time for them, don't worry. You don't even have to have your own. There's a surplus right now, in fact, globally. I was 19 when I got married the first time, and I'll be 38 the second. She'll be 27, or eight years older than I was the first time I got married. I think both of us know who we are now much more than I did at 19. And I think that's the key: if you can grow together and change enough then you'll be OK. If you're not compatible to begin with or fail to adapt to the changes in the other person, you'll fail. But it's OK to fail. However, given that I made it 17 years with the wrong person, I feel like the chances are pretty, pretty good that I made the right decision this time around.

And we've been through some shit together, don't get me wrong. I've been manic during her depressions and made some super impulsive decisions with long-lasting consequences, and I've hurt her terribly in the past. And I'm not saying she hasn't done anything to me, either, but it takes a special person to be in a relationship with a bipolar person. You have to be able to draw some clear boundaries of what you'll tolerate before you have to commit them—or worse, leave them altogether. My ex-wife tried to do that with me and asked me to get (almost) entirely sober (including drugs, alcohol, and tobacco, but especially weed). She never understood or believed (I'm not sure which) that it truly helps me regulate my bipolar disorder. And, in part because of that irreconcilable difference (and many others), we parted ways amicably. My fiancée actually gets how weed helps me manage my disorder, though. Be still, my beating heart!

So one of the funny ironies about me is that I am a professional mediator, but I get in fights all the time. Not (necessarily) physical ones, but I *can* be a bit abrasive at times, which can (and often does) lead to conflict. Sometimes I actually enjoy arguing with friends of mine who I know can handle a good debate. I honestly think they're fun. But I'm the "lawyer-type" personality on Meyers-Briggs, so I'm ruthless in the "courtroom" of relationship battles. Which, I've learned, is not always appreciated by my partner. Now, what I'm going to tell you about fights next will come from the mediator-hat-wearing side of me. The transformative mediator, to be precise. In the transformative approach to conflict, the whole theory basically boils down to the key propositions that conflict is a "crisis in human interaction," and that it is made worse by the fact that we operate out of weakness and self-absorption while we are in it. In other words, fights happen because we are unable to communicate effectively and when they do, we get big mad and petty, which makes things worse. This, in turn, leads to a downward spiral that we can easily get sucked into, never to return. So, not great.

The opposite of weakness and self-absorption, then, is strength and connection. This is the side of you that thinks "maybe we can talk through it," and wants to restore the relationship. It's also the side of you willing to see their side, and willing to try and change your behavior when you need to. Most importantly, however, it's the side of you that's willing to listen. That's the side you need to tap into when things are at their worst. But I can tell you, even as a mediator, being in conflict sucks, and you really can't mediate your own disputes. You have to work through the situation together or get someone else to help you.

What you can do, however, is focus on listening. You can reflect and summarize what they're saying to make sure you understand their point of view. You can stay open instead of closed off. You can choose to engage instead of shutting down. You can write your thoughts down in a journal instead of shouting them at one another (or silently bottling them all up inside), and then give the journals to each other to read when you're both feeling less heated. You can learn how to argue better. You can realize that it's both of you against the issue instead of both of you versus each other. All of those things are within your power, if you choose to do them.

Or, you can blame them and refuse to take responsibility. You can also become toxic and bring up their past transgressions as a way to "win" an argument. You can even use their deepest insecurities against them. Or you can simply walk away. All of these are also within your power. I've tried all of these as well, and I can say definitively that they do not work. Not even a little bit. Unless you're trying to end the relationship, then they work great. But that's not what I wanted and, thankfully, that's not what the SLF wanted, either, so we fight for our relationship every day and we are stronger because of it.

But if you were to ask the SLF (or the ex), I'm sure they could both tell you about the unique challenges that come with being in an intimate relationship with a bipolar person like myself. And they are plentiful. One is that sometimes our brains take over and we can no longer do those things I mentioned above, and we start down a self-destructive path that (potentially) only a hospitalization can pull us out of. Meanwhile, we'll only go kicking and screaming and refuse to believe our friends and loved ones when they tell us we're (quite literally) out of our minds. But even in less dramatic scenarios we can be difficult. Sometimes, for example, our mania takes over and causes us to want to go on a spending spree that you have to curtail diplomatically. Or maybe we get some grand new business idea, and you have to be the bad guy for asking for things like a "business plan" before any funds are dedicated to it. Or maybe our depression means we can't be there emotionally for you for a while.

All of these scenarios can be extremely difficult and lead to hurtful fights if you're not careful, so it's important to come up with a preliminary agreement on when you'll decide to get treatment and what will happen when you're manic (or depressed) and want to start (or end) something big in your life. The mania contract and suicide safety plan I've included in the appendix are both good places to start that discussion. The benefit of this, of course, is that if there's already a process in place that you both believe is fair when challenges like these comes along, there doesn't have to be an argument (at least, that's the theory…). I promise, this can save you a lot of future heartache. Talk about as many scenarios as you can before they happen and agree on something when you're both of sound mind. You won't regret it, I promise. And you might even save your future relationship by taking these proactive steps.

# **Chapter 7**



*Dealing with Fascists and Hospitalizations*

As I've mentioned before, one of the nearly thirty jobs I've had over the years was being a professional mediator. I worked for the City of Dayton Mediation Center helping people resolve disputes of all kinds. One time I even helped two mediators try and work things out. It was interesting. But during the course of that job my boss wanted me to work with the local police on a project, so I signed up for a ride-along to get a better sense of how mediation might be useful. It didn't take too much convincing on my end that an unarmed communications expert could do more to defuse a situation than a cop... I think the police should be abolished anyways. But that's for another book.

During one of the ride-alongs, I had an exchange that I'll never forget. "What's the most common complaint you guys have to respond to?" I asked. "Oh, definitely mental health crises," he explained without hesitating. Now, if that's not a reason to divert some funding from the police to social workers in and of itself, I don't know what is. But unfortunately, most places haven't done that just yet. So, the reality is that you're likely to run into a fucking fascist at some point if you're not careful. Particularly if you're bipolar, and *especially* if you're bipolar 1. So how does one stay out of Malibu, deadbeat? Preparation is pretty important, if you ask my opinion. Which I guess you did, since you're reading this.

Before I get too far into the prep side, however, let me just give you an idea of how bad it can get. I checked myself into the hospital during my last full-blown mania episode because I was so delusional that I thought my boss was a spy and that I had blown her cover and the only way to help her out was by checking myself into the hospital and telling them I was going to kill myself. Now, was I *seriously* thinking of killing myself? No, that usually happens more when I'm depressed. But, I did know that it would get me admitted. And I don't think my ex was capable of handling me by that point, anyways. Staying up all night smoking Churchill-length cigars in the living room with a friend until 5AM one time was enough for her. So, I checked myself in.

Now I was completely gone at this point. I remember watching *Ellen* in the room they put me in and somehow convincing myself that the "holding cell" (for lack of a better term) that I was in was actually her green room, and that I was going to be called on as a guest at any moment and given a medal by the president for my great work uncovering an international sex trafficking ring. But at one point I was getting a little restless and wanted to get on stage sooner rather than later, so I started banging on the doors. Two of the hospital police showed up and (in my mind) I merely asked them if they wanted to do some jiu-jitsu. I'm a blue belt, and they looked like they enjoyed a good roll, so I was just looking for a way to pass the time. And no, I'm really not making that up, I wasn't actually trying to take out the cops, I truly was just looking for something to do. They saw it differently, however, and that's how I got put on my second 72-hour hold. In some municipalities they call this being "pink slipped," so named for the pink slip they used to use when you'd get admitted. A pink slip isn't quite like getting arrested, but for all intents and purposes, you are essentially locked up against your will. You're at the mercy of the doctors or the legal system to let you out at that point, and it's a terrifying thing. Some people use the legal system to get free while other people learn to play nice with the doctors to get let out. I've tried both, and I can tell you without a doubt, the second option is superior. Yes, you're locked up. But it's much nicer than jail (I've been there, too, it's much more dreary). So, I want to share some tips in case it ever happens to you.

For starters, write your name on your underwear. Yes, people do steal things (and they're not big on locked doors in the psych ward), so labeling your stuff is very helpful in case it happens and you know who took it, which is the case more often than you might expect. Don't worry though about your socks, you'll get cool new grippy ones anyways. And that leads me to my second piece of advice about your stay at the grippy socks hotel: just look at it like a vacation. Except unlike the Hotel California, it doesn't have to be the case that once you check in, you can never leave. And thank fuck for that, because I hate the fucking Eagles, man. But, I mean, it's probably going to cost you as much as a month-long European trip, so you might as well live it up, right? Just imagine: your food is catered, you get a decent bed, 24/7 round-the-clock care, usually there are games and TV (although a curfew might be enforced), and oftentimes there are fun workshops you can attend. I've done some of my best artwork while in the psych ward (in my humble opinion). My favorite is when we do music classes, though. Those rock.

*I just thought we were going to roll a little bit... I wasn't trying to be a threat, officer, I promise.*

Hands down, though, the best part is having no cell phone. You didn't think they'd let you keep that, did you? But look at it as a blessing. Where else have you truly not had to worry about responding to texts and emails for 72 hours? I've never even had that much freedom on a vacation. It's truly the last place you can check into and check out and not worry about anyone but yourself. Honestly, you should be paying them for holding you. Oh wait, nevermind, you are. Make sure you have insurance, by the way, or it may result in crippling debt. More on that in another chapter, though.

That being said, staying out of the psych ward is always a much better alternative. Looking at it positively is good, sure, but better never to have to be locked up at all. But how does one stay out of the psych ward during a manic episode, you ask? It's not easy, but there are a lot of things you can do to improve the odds that you'll never be inside of one. All of them have in common, however, that you really need to institute those safeguards *before* you're too manic to think straight. Otherwise, you're not going to make the right decisions.

One thing I'd recommend is coming up with a literal contract and signing it. I have one with my fiancée and it includes a list of symptoms and a number of bullet points representing agreements I've made that I will do in the event that those symptoms begin to rear their ugly heads. They include things like being in bed by 1AM and sleeping for at least six hours per night, taking my prescribed meds (including ones I only take when the mania gets really bad), making no investment decisions, and not spending over $30 per day when I'm manic (without approval). Oh, and this is huge, but I agree to have my phone taken away when things get too bad. You might think this is dumb, but part of the problem with mania is that you begin to see connections between everything, and texting with people and having internet access that allows you to research those seven new business ideas you just came up with can be a huge accelerant for your racing thoughts. So, things like reading or watching TV are good, as it's less about screen time and more about not allowing your brain to run off on its own and get you into trouble. Add in the fact that bipolar people are stereotypically considered (even if for good reason) to be more likely to cheat on their partners, and it really just gives everyone more peace of mind. You can find a reproduction of our contract in the appendix that you can make your own, and I highly suggest you do so.

Which brings me to another point; and that is that putting these safeguards in place isn't just for you. It's for your friends and family, as well. Your behavior can become truly traumatizing for others if you're not managing your care, so it's crucial to create expectations about what will happen when you're manic (and clearly outlining at what point you'll go to the doctor and/or hospital — for me, it's experiencing hallucinations and delusions). That step is crucial for maintaining a semblance of control over the situation for you and your partner(s), friends, and/or family members. I promise you'll thank me later, and they'll thank you for doing it.

Of course, putting a contract in place is one thing; following it is another. This is why it's important to be accurate about the symptoms you experience (and recognize that they can and do change over time, and even vary from one episode to another), so look at it more as a living document and less as an inalterable constitution with inalienable rights. Even more important, however, is the attitude you have about it. After my first hospitalization, I denied that I was bipolar. After my second one, however, I accepted it and put these safeguards in place. I haven't been back since (knock on wood), but I have definitely been manic since then. Thankfully I'm no longer afraid of going to the psych ward if I have to, I just recognize that it's a very expensive stay and I should do everything I can to avoid it (but I should go if I need to be there). But having that mindset of no longer being afraid of going (and recognizing that it's temporary if I do) has made me free to be much more honest with myself and others about whether it's time to go or not.

Part of not being afraid, though, is also finding a place you want to be taken. My first stay was awful, in part, because of the staff at that facility. The staff at the second one I went to wasn't nearly as bad. For example, they don't let you have caffeine, and after two days of being there I recognized I was being served decaf the whole time and had a crushing headache. The staff took pity on me and gave me some real coffee. Now, that's where I'll go any time I need to be hospitalized. If nothing else, I'm a loyal customer, OK?

Now, there are places you can go to look up reviews of psych wards (such as Facebook and Reddit) before you have to go. So, I'd recommend doing a little Googling on the ones in your area while your mood is stable, so that when the time comes, you'll at least know which ones to avoid. Better yet, get into a bipolar support group and ask others where the best places are to visit. You'll be glad you did, as our mental healthcare system is less of a system and more of a patchwork quilt of care sewn together by people of widely varying skill levels. The point being, of course, that not all psych wards are created equally. Nor are psychiatrists, for that matter. They should honestly be doing everything they can to keep you out of there, so if yours isn't, then find a new one that you're comfortable with. It will save you a lot of time, heartache, and money. And speaking of money and planning ahead, let's talk about finances next.

# Chapter 8



*Dealing with Spending Habits while Manic*

When you're manic, money is quite literally no object. You see no reason to save money and every reason to spend it. This phenomenon could be called "bipolar math," and it's all too real, unfortunately. Allow me to give you just a couple of oh-so many examples. These are just the ones I (hopefully) miraculously escaped from.

The year was 2022, and I was going through a divorce while dating the person who is now my fiancée. I had just decided I didn't want to move to Bosnia and Herzegovina after all. Instead, I wanted to see where things went with my situationship. But I didn't have a house and was living in a pull-behind camper. Coincidentally, it's worth mentioning that I bought that travel trailer at the height of my mania *and* the height of the used camper market, as everyone was anxious to travel during Covid. And, as a result, it's now worth less than half of what I paid for it. But that's the least of the bad decisions I made in this story. Say what you will about it, it was a nice place to live. I just needed a stable place to park it, as I had been using an app called Harvest Host to find places to stay. It was great, as it allowed me to stay at a bunch of places for the low price of just buying some stuff from the breweries, wineries, and farms where I parked. The only downside was having to move the camper every day, as you were only allowed to stay in any one place a maximum of 24 hours.

So, I found some land for sale that wasn't too far from her place. Now, it's also important to note that one of my manic ideas (that I haven't given up on) was to start a Dudeist Retreat Center. And this is probably as good a good place as any to point out that not all manic ideas are bad ones. It's just not the ideal time to make huge life-altering decisions. Maybe if this book does well, I'll get enough seed money to start it, though. But the whole idea was to find a beautiful, wooded area that I could park my camper at and live full time while building the retreat, which would have a large hall for hosting gatherings and shows and art displays and workshops on everything from birdwatching to how to infuse food with weed. It would also have a number of small shacks for people to stay in while they were visiting. I would then chronicle me building them on my YouTube channel, of course.

Now this isn't all that far-fetched. I've already built a couple of these "tiny house shacks," as I like to call them, and the place I found for my retreat was perfect, (or so I thought at the time). It had about 2.5 acres of woods, a giant parking area, tons of amazing birds (I love birdwatching), and an historic old barn that I could repurpose into that retreat center. The only problem was that it was listed for $100,000, when it should have been listed for about $50,000.

But, as I have alluded to, money is no object when you're manic. And you also suffer from a kind of thinking where you believe if you don't act fast, then opportunities are going to slip away. So I found a friend who was a realtor and offered full price, with no inspections. Needless to say, they accepted my offer (there's a manic sucker born every minute, they probably thought). But after a night where I got so drunk that I Ubered 45 minutes home to a camper that had no heat in the dead of winter (and no power to charge my dead phone), I realized I was a little too manic. It wasn't until then that I started to wonder if what I planned to do with the property was even legal (a little late in the game, but a good thought, nonetheless). So, I went to the county engineer's office and, yada yada yada, found out that I wouldn't be able to legally do any of the things I wanted to with the property without a variance from the township's board of trustees. So, I panicked.

I quietly removed my camper from the property and got my motorcycle off the land as well, then I dipped out of the sales process entirely, leaving it to my realtor to let the sellers know that I was backing out. Thinking that was the end of it, I congratulated myself (prematurely, I soon learned) on getting out of a terrible manic land deal just in time. Little did I know that, technically, I had breached a contract, allowing them to sue me for the difference between market price and what I had offered. Not only that, the statute of limitations on it was six years! So, I don't know how this story ends just yet, but after some extremely nasty Facebook messages I sent, they accepted my offer of $750 in earnest money that I hoped would settle things, and I'm hoping that's the end of it. Only time will tell, however.

*The "$100,000" property that I briefly lived on before abandoning the deal… it would have made a great Dudeist Retreat Center location though!*

Now, this is just the largest dollar amount I ever (almost) spent while manic, but there are tens (if not hundreds) of similar smaller stories just like it. Shortly thereafter, in fact, I got it in my head that I wanted to become a travel agent. Once again, it wasn't a super far-fetched notion. I have taken over 50 people back and forth between Dayton and Bosnia-Herzegovina, so I thought having a niche travel business charging people for that sort of service would be a good idea. So, I incorporated a business (in case you want to go). However, after watching one YouTube video that convinced me to virtually attend a free online intro course, I was ready to sign up for their months-long "school" to get certified as a travel agent. Now I don't think this company is illegitimate, exactly, I just think they're a bit predatory, as they charged $6,000 for the package. After learning of this, my (now) fiancée sighed, and I knew I had fucked up again. I did everything I could to get my money back, but I had signed a contract and provided them with my credit card information, so they'd already taken my $1000 down payment. Panicking, I took the approach of being as crazy as possible. I emailed and called them repeatedly asking for my money back or to go to mediation, wrote horrible reviews all over their social media accounts, and told them that I wasn't in my right mind when entering the contract and would be suing for the return of my funds. Shockingly, it worked. But it was far too close of a call.

The funny thing is that normally I'm *not* terrible with money. I have an "excellent" credit rating with all three credit bureaus, because I pay my bills on time and use debt responsibly. I've even had some business ideas that have worked out, if you can believe it. All that goes out the window, however, when I'm manic. Now I will admit that I always like spending money, but I'm far less cautious about how much I actually have when I'm manic. Couple that (last year) with going through a divorce and having my ex-wife buy me out of my half of our house while I was selling a bunch of shit, and I suddenly had a ton of cash that was burning a hole not just in my pocket, but in my entire being. I *had* to spend money. I justified it any way that I could, including by trying to woo my situationship with nice trips and cruises. I just didn't let her know how fast the nest egg was being drained. And hey, I guess it worked, but I got lucky in that I had cash on hand and didn't have to go into debt.

I did at least do some "smart" things to mitigate my spending. And I would highly recommend this to others, as I know of a guy on TikTok who is well-known for spending $20,000 on crystals while manic in the hopes that he could sell them and start a business. He now has an amazing crystal collection and a lot of followers, but that's about it. I, on the other hand, had learned my lesson (to some extent), and I spent my money (mostly) on, either, experiences I'd always wanted to have or things I could later resell. The camper is a great example of this. I also bought a truck to tow it. Are they now worth what I paid for them? Absolutely not. I sold the truck for less than half of what I bought it for and the camper is still up for grabs as of the time of this writing, but at least I have some ideas of what to do with it and a place to park it for now. I'm lucky, though, that I don't hugely regret everything I spent the money on, as not everyone who goes through one of these episodes can say that, unfortunately.

Now, you may or may not want to give up this much freedom, but there *are* financial tools out there that can potentially help you as well. I should note here that I am not a financial advisor, and that I highly recommend consulting one before pursuing any of the ideas I'm going to share. But, one of those financial tools at your disposal is a trust, in particular a "spendthrift trust." The basic idea behind any trust is that you're putting money away for someone to use in the future. This could be for many reasons, but one of those reasons is if you are not mature enough, or don't trust yourself enough to manage it on your own. A spendthrift trust is designed specifically for those reasons. They're often used to pass down an inheritance to someone who is immature, so that they don't blow it all at once (hence the derogatory term "trust fund kids"). Unfortunately, when you're manic, you're really not much different than a spoiled 15-year-old kid when it comes to spending or investing for the future. This type of trust, however, can be managed by a trustee you know and have confidence in (whether they be a close friend or a family member). It can be set up to be disbursed at their discretion, or you could set it up to provide a certain amount at set intervals, such as monthly payouts. This could be a good option for you, particularly if you have a lot of assets to protect.

Let's say, however, that you can't afford to set up a trust, or don't have enough money to make one relevant. That means it's actually *more* important, in all likelihood, that you do something to slow down your mania-induced carefree spending habits, because a manic money-spending adventure is going to hurt your wallet a whole lot more. So, what I would recommend would be to simply hand over all of the keys to your money to someone you know and trust, but who is also able to tell you "no." By "keys to your money," I mean your credit and debit cards, the passwords to all your online banking platforms (including your Venmo, PayPal, and CashApp accounts), and probably even your bank-accepted forms of ID. Now you might perhaps be thinking, "why would I give up my ID, Arch?" Well, I'll tell you why. It's because eventually you're going to go down to the bank in person for the first time since before the pandemic and withdraw money that way, bypassing all of your other safeguards. And because you don't have a trust, they'll have to give it to you. So, give them your IDs, too, because the manic version of you is much wilier and more determined than you could ever imagine (if you haven't gone manic yet). And, as they say – where there's a will, there's a way. So don't give yourself the option and make sure there's no way for you to access your money without your trusted other signing off on it.

Of course, you might be saying, "but Arch, I need to pay for stuff still," and you'd be right. My solution? Let's just go find a cash machine and use hard currency for everything. Or pre-paid credit cards, if you just can't handle using cash. But either way, the point is for your most trusted significant other to allow you as much as you need to get through the week (or day, depending on how severe your mania is and how compulsive your purchasing becomes). Kind of like an allowance, if you will. Sure, it's annoying and impractical, but blowing all your money on your "amazing idea" of starting an online shoe and costume rental business for aspiring clowns is going to be much less devastating over the long run than not having enough money for that iced latte because you spent it already on a dozen pretzels from the bakery you like to frequent to give to the homeless people you've recently befriended at your local park. Trust me. These are warnings that are born out of experience, here.

But what happens when you get that amazing business idea that you just *know* is going to earn you tens of thousands of dollars (at the very least)? And trust me, if you're manic and consider yourself to be even remotely creative and/or have some business acumen, you'll come up with a business idea. I have two LLCs that can attest to that fact. Here's my advice though. For starters, recognize that it may or may not be a good idea, but regardless of whether it is or not, now is not the time to go fully into execution mode and start a brand new business venture.

What I've learned to do, instead, is to see how far I can get with an idea before I absolutely have to spend money on it. Or, better yet, I make my goal to spend $0 on a project unless I absolutely have to, and only then with my fiancée's approval (which isn't easy to get). It's important to recognize, though, that bipolar people are very creative, and they see connections sometimes that other people don't. If you have an idea (like I had an idea to write this book), then by all means go after it. Just don't spend any money. Or only spend whatever is absolutely necessary. But keep in mind that bartering is often more valuable than spending money on something. I wrote this entire book and published it without spending a dime. I'm not joking. My brother is a writer, so I got him to agree to edit the book on the hope of a future commission. I also had a TikTok friend help me with the graphic arts for the cover (thank you @MaryTheadoor of TikTok!). Then I self-published it using a pay-as-you-print model that required no funds up front, and doing the ebook and audiobook versions on my own. I'm doing all of the marketing myself because I used to be in marketing, and so I never had to spend a penny. It's not always the case that you have to spend money to make money.

But whether I make any money or not is irrelevant. The important thing is that I completed a project/idea I had that I'm passionate about without spending any money, even though I was manic several times throughout the process. I have learned over time that good ideas have a way of becoming a reality with or without me spending my own money on them, for the most part. So, find creative solutions and use your manic energy to plan and strategize so that when your mood comes back down, you're left with a blueprint for success instead of a lot of unpaid bills with nothing to show for them.

To use another example, I built a little "tiny house office," (as I like to call it) in my backyard during the pandemic. It was so fun I wanted to do it again. This time, however, I built a little shack down in the woods of southern Ohio. I spent little to no money on it, as I salvaged most of the necessary materials for free. One day I just decided I was going to build it without spending money, and I slowly started gathering what I needed. I found some old lumber my grandpa didn't need for flooring. A roofer was getting rid of some unused shingles for a job, which I took. I found an old door in an alley. My friend Mike (who has a really cool YouTube channel called *A Cabin and Fifty Acres*, which I can't recommend enough) had some old 2x4s that I framed it up with. Honestly, doing it that way was more fun, as well. Advertising my YouTube channel is also what got me onto TikTok, where I now have 12,000 people who follow my account for some reason or another, and I'm very grateful for each and every one of them who does. But none of that would have happened if I had decided to just spend money on building a shack in the woods. So put it out there in the universe and see how far you can get sans money. You won't regret it.

Another thing you won't regret is all of the money you saved by not rushing into a business venture while you're manic. Sometimes I compare bipolar disorder to a thief in the night, because it can steal so many things from you. Friends, family members, careers, and significant others are all likely victims. But so is your literal cash. So, protect yourself from manic you and make sure you have put whatever safeguards in place you need in order to secure your cash.

Now that we've talked about protecting your cash, let's move on to another topic: how to ensure you maintain your ability to make more of it.

5 8

# Chapter 9

## Are You Employed, Sir?

*Working with Bipolar*

There are millionaires who are bipolar and homeless people who are bipolar. The major difference between the two is how much money they have. Some of them are leading entire nations, while others are collecting social security benefits. You might even be at both ends of the spectrum in a single lifetime. But unless you are born into or inherit a great deal of wealth, which end of the poverty-to-millionaire spectrum you end up closer to will, unfortunately (in our cruelly self-help capitalist US society, at least), be largely dependent upon your ability to build your own wealth through providing something of value to others *or* upon your ability to access and draw upon the very meager social safety nets our country has put in place for people such as us. I'm here to tell you there's no shame in whatever path you choose.

I choose to try and work, mostly because I want to maintain a certain lifestyle and, unfortunately, disability doesn't quite cover it. You would make about $20,000 on disability benefits (if you're lucky), and they are notoriously difficult to secure. Not only that, you essentially have to agree not to work for the rest of your life, at least to go on the public employee disability system in my state, that is. The moment you start working, your benefits are in jeopardy. I've spent about seven years of my life teaching high school, and five years working in public service, and about four years teaching college courses. I was very close to filing for benefits on several occasions, but every time I did, I stopped short, because I love teaching, and I'd have to give that up if I decided to collect disability. It's shitty, but that's America for you.

My first manic episode came just a year into my teaching career, but I was able to recover from it and went on in a year or two to become the Ohio Council for the Social Studies' Emerging Educator of the Year, which was a pretty high honor as a young teacher. I went on from there and ran for office and got elected to serve as the Vice President of my hometown's board of education while simultaneously earning my master's in international and comparative politics. I was also a regular at national conferences presenting on a range of topics, and after five years of successful classroom teaching, I moved into a pseudo-administrative role as a community outreach director. I excelled in that position, as well, helping the school increase enrollment and create its first-ever strategic plan, which has positioned it to now become the number one school in the Dayton area. After that, I decided to switch careers entirely and become a professional mediator, which I had been doing as a volunteer for about a year. I also became treasurer, vice chair, then chair of my city's sister city committee, and vice president of the local council on world affairs. I did well academically too, never getting below an A in my entire graduate school career and being recognized as the Outstanding College of Liberal Arts Student of the Year *and* Outstanding Graduate Student of the Year. I did all of this while managing a successful business on the side. In short, I was one of Dayton's own Little Lebowski Urban Achievers.

*Me proudly displaying my "Emerging Leader" award from the Ohio Council for the Social Studies.*

*One of my proudest accomplishments while I worked for the city was writing and managing a $120,000 US Department of State grant that brought 17 students and three teachers from Bosnia and Herzegovina to Dayton, OH.*

Let's stop and talk about quitting your job for a moment, though, because it's a pretty common thing for bipolar people to do. What I would say first is this: don't quit your job if you can help it. Not having income is stressful, and stress isn't great for your bipolar, so if there's any way you can hold onto it, I would always lean towards trying to do that. But sometimes you just can't imagine yourself going on in the same position. In those cases, I think you have to ask yourself, "if I was functioning at 100% and my mood was stable, would I be able to do this job well?" If the answer is yes, I would do everything I could to keep my position. Go on FMLA, or even go on an unpaid leave of absence. But whatever you do, make them fire *you*, don't fire yourself. Otherwise, you can't collect unemployment benefits.

Now, you might be thinking, "I would never quit my job if I was bipolar," and I love that for you. But unfortunately, bipolar people can be a bit impulsive at times, so they don't always think through their decisions all the way. Catch us on a bad day and, like George Costanza, we might just chew you out and quit because you took our favorite work-shitting location and turned it into your own private restroom.

My job-quitting tendency typically is at its peak, however, when I'm depressed. I begin to think there's no way I'll ever be able to do my job and that I'm just dead weight and I don't deserve to have the position I hold. Add in a bit of imposter's syndrome and a dash of midlife crisis and that's how I ended up quitting at least three different full-time positions that all had nice benefits, healthcare, and pretty decent salaries. So it goes.

After leaving mediation behind, I embarked upon a journey of trying to figure out what I truly wanted to do with my life. My biggest problem, of course, is that I just don't like working. I don't understand people who get off on it at all. I would have to agree with James Baldwin (and the corresponding TikTok meme) when he said, "Darling, I have no dream job; I do not dream of labor." That would summarize my sentiments precisely. Unless being the new Anthony Bourdain is on the table, then I'd reconsider. That being said, some jobs are certainly more tolerable, at least, than others, and few years ago I set out on a quest to find jobs I actually wanted to do.

Initially, I thought I could go back to being a server while being a doorman on the side. I made it about two weeks at Applebee's before their Stone Age POS (aka point of sale/piece of shit) system ended up pissing me off so much one day that I left and never went back. I enjoyed my bouncing gig at a local bar, but that was only two days a week, and the hours weren't great. After that I decided to try to become a woodworker, which I've always loved to do. I realized pretty quickly, however, that doing it to make money is really an entirely different ball game, and I wasn't prepared to spend 50% of my time on marketing, nor did I have the skills to really make the kind of pieces that would actually sell. After that I tried pizza delivery for Domino's and made it a whole half day there; a new record for me in terms of least time spent at a job, just barely edging out the single day I spent as a roofer. I did do DoorDash for a while, though, and I genuinely didn't mind that. It reminded me of the job I used to have reading electric meters back in college, only it was easier. I'll return more to that in a moment.

Eventually, I found a job working with a friend as an electrical assembler. You might be wondering "what's an electrical assembler?" Truth be told, I didn't even know that's what it was called when I first started. I just knew that they put together wiring harnesses that went into industrial dishwashers. In terms of being a good fit for my bipolar, it had several things going for it. For one, it was pretty low stress. Most of our days were spent watching movies while we crimped wires. Most importantly, I was working with a friend of mine who I enjoyed being around, and I realized that was pretty special. I settled into doing that and bouncing for a while, but I got tired of it after a few months. I also got a new job, which I wasn't really sold on, but which paid better than anything I'd ever done before: being a positive school climate coach for Dayton Public Schools.

*Pretty sure this is one of only two items I sold while I tried to make money as a woodworker.*

I have to admit that at first, I thought *perhaps* I'd be able to do the job fairly well. Essentially, it consisted of coaching other teachers on how to improve their practice. I thought I might do well at it because I'm a pretty decent teacher, after all, and I like working with other teachers. What I didn't know, however, was that they had a very specific idea in mind for what they meant by "coaching," and it all revolved around a book that they described as their "bible," and which prescribed a very rigid approach to classroom management. But in addition to trying to coach high school teachers to be the kind of teacher I never was, they also wanted me to work with elementary school teachers. And it wasn't just working with elementary school teachers, either. They often would just use our department to plug any kind of "hole" they had. One week we were fielding phone calls from angry parents about why the busses hadn't picked up their children, and the next we were subbing for teachers all across the district. I was in a different school every day and I hated my time at all of them.

I lasted about six months there before I quit, although that wasn't the end of my troubles. I also learned that the State of Ohio allows districts to revoke the teaching licenses of teachers who leave their district midyear for up to a full year, and they attempted to do just that to me. Fortunately, I was able to convince them that I had left for mental health reasons (which was true) thanks to my doctor writing me a note… but it didn't really matter. It would still be over a year before I set foot in a high school classroom once more.

After that, I decided to try and make money by podcasting. I even went to a podcasting conference out in Texas and learned everything I could about it. I was posting very consistently and slowly building my audience, but you really need at least six months to start to make money, if not one to two years. I quit at right about the six-month mark, right before deciding I was going to get a divorce and move to Bosnia and Herzegovina. That didn't go as planned, of course, either, and I ended up getting the divorce but meeting someone here before I left, falling in love, and deciding not to move overseas, after all. This solved my relationship problems, but it didn't do much for my career (or lack thereof) situation.

So, after simply not working for a while and running down my savings to next to nothing, I finally realized I needed to bring some money in if I wanted to maintain my lifestyle. Then, in January of 2022, I heard about a new charter school that was in its first year and looking for a social studies teacher midyear. I should have known that was a red flag, and if I'm being honest, I *did* know that. I just didn't know how bad it would be. One thing I have come to learn about education is that the school's leadership sets the tone for everything, and they do so regardless of whether they are amazing or horrible at their jobs. All told, I made it through the duration of the year, but not without frequently calling in sick to take mental health days. It was pretty rough, especially because I had already decided that I didn't really want to teach high school anymore. It's really fucking hard work. But I got health insurance for a while and banked a decent amount of money, and I like to think I did OK even, given the circumstances. I was able to help them do their first integrated project-based learning unit, for example, and I got many students to pass courses they never wanted to take, so I can still sleep OK at night.

After leaving there, however, I decided to just own the whole "part-time" thing and settled into trying to get as many college courses to teach as possible. I managed to get hired on as an adjunct lecturer at my alma mater as well, where I now teach an intro political science course that I really enjoy. Then I found a job where I am responsible for being the local housing manager for a group of international exchange students and (mostly) am just responsible for doing monthly inspections of their units. I also started substitute teaching at a couple local districts and tutoring on the side. Finally, I landed a job doing trivia one night a week at a local bar. I still DoorDash on occasion, as well. All this combined makes it possible for me to make my goal income of around $40-50K per year, and I'm pretty OK with that. I should add that I also have some side hustles that I haven't really been able to get going. One is leading people on trips to Bosnia and Herzegovina. Another is being a wedding officiant. And another one I am trying to get going is divorce mediation. None of these have really taken off, unfortunately, but my hope is that now that my work situation is a bit more stable and predictable, I'll be able to have the time needed to actually devote to one (or more) of these ideas and see if I can get them off the ground.

I give you this long work history so that you'll better understand many of the challenges I've experienced in my working life over the years as I've struggled to balance my mental health with earning an income. What I've learned through it all, though, is that I need my work life to be at least somewhat personally fulfilling, and it has to be flexible enough so that a manic or depressive episode don't derail it entirely. Also, the less of it I have to do, the better. One of the unfortunate truths that my working life and my friendships have in common is that I've burned a lot of bridges over the years in both areas. There are more than a few former employers who I know won't take me back because I wasn't in a good place mentally when I left, or I left impulsively due to a depressive episode (I rarely leave jobs when I'm manic). Unfortunately, this includes the only real mediation gig in town, and my favorite high school I've ever worked at, so the two jobs that have been most fulfilling in my life are essentially ruled out for me. So having multiple jobs (and, by extension, multiple bosses) is a coping tactic I use in a manner that's similar to my friendships, whereby I try not to burn myself or others out too much at any one place. Instead, I have several jobs, so when the bar cancels trivia (which they did recently) I can pick up more hours subbing or doing DoorDash a little more.

More than that, though, being a jack of all trades also just helps ensure I don't get too bored. I'd say I have my teaching jobs down to where I can teach five classes per semester and work maybe one full day per week (unless I have a lot of grading to do). My tutoring gigs take maybe a full half day per week, as well. I only really work for a few hours per month on the housing gig. And (when it was happening regularly) trivia is only a couple hours per week. This is especially helpful because my fiancée has a number of health problems that mean I need to stay flexible and available for her when it comes to my own schedule. But it also gives me time to work on my projects, like restarting my podcasts and writing this book.

The freedom and peace of mind that comes with having more time is invaluable, I've found, for my mental health. If I'm manic or depressed, an entire day at work from 8AM-5PM can be incredibly draining. But I can almost always manage to teach a couple classes on my busy days, knowing that I can rest the next day. I have also noticed, (and maybe this is a bipolar thing, or a latent ADHD thing, or is perhaps just part of my personality), that I get very bored doing the same thing day in and day out, and having each day be something different is something that just keeps me much more interested in the jobs I'm doing. And having flexible work options that I can literally do whenever I want, such as DoorDash, make it much easier to capitalize on the times that I'm feeling good. Plus, I really kind of love just being alone in my car and driving around picking up and dropping off food while listening to music, podcasts, and audio books. It doesn't get much better, to be honest. So, I guess my advice would be to look into the gig economy or self-employment options if you're bipolar. There are a lot of other jobs you can do, though, that work well for someone with bipolar disorder. One of my TikTok friends finds that being a realtor helps him achieve a balance fairly well as a bipolar person given its flexible nature. But find what works for you best. The only real downside (and this is really just true for Americans) is that you don't get health insurance benefits. But you can (and I would argue should, if you can afford it) purchase it on the private market and make it work that way. If you're lucky like me and happen to be in pretty decent physical health, bipolar isn't a terribly expensive illness, either. I guess I should say that comes with one big caveat, which is that it's not expensive *unless you have to go into the hospital*. Then it becomes ridiculously expensive very quickly. But if you can manage to stay out of grippy socks jail, then buying your own insurance isn't going to break the bank if you're working, and if you're not then you should definitely get on Medicaid.

All that being said, you have to figure out what works best for you, sometimes through trial and error. It's also true that for bipolar people, routine can be very important and something you should strive for. I've not found that to be entirely true for me, but for some friends, I know they do benefit from the regimented life that comes with a full-time job, and that's great for them. But even if you do choose to go the gig route, you can still build in plenty of routine into your day, and it's probably a good idea to do so, at least to some extent. The goal is to find what works best for you, and ultimately only you can know what that is. Hopefully, though, this gives you a bit of an insight into what might be worth trying.

# Chapter 10



## What Condition my Condition Is In

*How to Tell When You're Manic or Depressed and Live a Complete Life*

It often comes as a surprise to people, but I frequently don't know what mood I'm in. And it's not just me, I would say that every bipolar person I know often finds it difficult to say for sure if they're experiencing whatever mood they think they're experiencing. This is especially true for mania, but it's even true of depression. That's partly because the changes in your mood or behavior can be so imperceptible and the symptoms so benign (or seemingly "normal") that it becomes difficult to know whether or not you did something because you were using regular thought processes, or because you need to up your meds. This becomes especially difficult in relationships when your significant other knows what mood you're in and you don't. It can be very taxing trying to convince someone they're manic and not in the best headspace to make a $10,000 purchase on a new camper that they can't afford, especially when you share finances.

So how do you make it easier on them (and yourself) to recognize the symptoms of mania? For starters, make that contract I talked about earlier and explicitly give your significant other permission to tell you when they think you're going manic (or depressive) and forgo purchases until you're more stable. But you bear some responsibility, as well, especially if you're single. So how do you recognize the signs on your own? It's a bit of an art and a science, to be sure, but it starts with being familiar with the tell-tale signs of mania and depression and then having an understanding of how those symptoms manifest themselves in you when you're in one (or both) of those moods. And the stakes are kind of high, because the sooner you recognize the symptoms, the easier it'll be to deal with them. Many a hospitalization has happened because the bipolar person didn't recognize (or refused to believe) what their symptoms were telling them. Don't be like those bipolars. Be a smart bipolar. Be an achiever. Recognize the signs and act accordingly.

But what are the signs, you ask? Well, according to the Mayo Clinic, being in a state of hypomania or mania necessitates having at least three of the following symptoms simultaneously:

- *Abnormally upbeat, jumpy or wired*
- *Increased activity, energy or agitation*
- *Exaggerated sense of well-being and self-confidence (euphoria)*
- *Decreased need for sleep*
- *Unusual talkativeness*
- *Racing thoughts*
- *Distractibility*
- *Poor decision-making — for example, going on buying sprees, taking sexual risks or making foolish investments*[13]

They go on to add some additional signs, explaining that "Signs and symptoms of bipolar I and bipolar II disorders may include other features, such as anxious distress, melancholy, psychosis or others. The timing of symptoms may include diagnostic labels such as mixed or rapid cycling."[14]

All of these symptoms are ones you can self-monitor if you're willing to be a little introspective and brutally honest with yourself. Are you excited about everything or have a million different business ideas per day? You're probably a bit upbeat and have increased energy. Have trouble just focusing on one thing, or continuing to jump from one idea to the next and seeing connections everywhere? Sounds like racing thoughts. Are friends telling you that you seem talkative or chatty? You're probably super wired. Not going to bed until 4AM and then waking up at 7:30AM? That's not enough sleep, dude. Did you just invest $4,000 in an online training course to learn how to start a podcast? You're not making sound financial decisions. (And you should have come to me, I'm much cheaper.)

If you're bipolar I, you have to be especially careful, because there's almost no limit to the amount of "ramping up" one can do while manic. If left unchecked, you'll have yourself convinced that the Chinese government and the FBI are both after you and that your special lady friend needs to take you to a safe house because the radio is

---

[13] "Diseases & Conditions: Bipolar Disorder," The Mayo Clinic Staff, December 13, 2022, https://www.mayoclinic.org/diseases-conditions/bipolar-disorder/symptoms-causes/syc-20355955.
[14] Ibid.

broadcasting your every move and the people who are out to get you are closing in fast. Not that I speak from personal experience here or anything. But the real danger of bipolar I is when you become delusional and start to hallucinate. At that stage there's a very low probability that you're going to snap out of it yourself, and more likely than not you're going to have to go to the hospital. So learn to recognize the signs much sooner so as to avoid that.

One thing I do that some people might find strange when I think I'm becoming delusional is I say what I think is happening out loud around other people. It's a crude (but effective) way to check *my* reality against *actual* reality. I'll explain what I mean. Say, for example, that I think I've uncovered an international crime ring operating out of my workplace. Maybe I think one of my coworkers has just returned from a mission and is debriefing me. I'll actually say that out loud and gauge their reaction. If they look at me like I've just become a chia pet and have microgreens growing out of my head, then I'll take that to mean perhaps I'm misjudging the situation a bit. If, on the other hand, they confirm my thinking, I know I'm not too far gone. It might seem like a stupid thing, but honestly, it's far more stupid to think those things and not let anyone know what's really going on inside your head. That's where you get into trouble, especially if you're a great masker like I am. That's how I got into lots of trouble that time I masked so well that my ex came to work to get me and take me home because she knew I was too far gone, but my coworkers thought that *she* was the crazy one and actually banned her from my workplace. I checked myself into the hospital later that day. If they actually knew what was going on inside my head as I attempted to "work through" the mania, however, they would never have let me step foot inside the building.

Another tactic I use frequently is empirical data. Sometimes you simply don't think you have an issue because you don't see the obvious. Recognizing the obvious, however, can be a huge asset when you're struggling with a manic episode, in particular. Look at your credit card statements. Are there huge jumps in spending? Where is all of the money going? If there's been a large expense like having to replace your furnace or something like that, OK. But if nothing out of the ordinary has happened and your spending went up by $3,000 in one month, you've got a problem, dude. Similarly, you are able to operate seemingly forever on just a couple hours of sleep while you're manic, so start tracking your sleep (if you don't do that already). Doctors will tell you that sleep is the number one most important thing to do when you're manic, and they're right, unfortunately. If you find yourself regularly getting only two to three hours of shut eye per night, just know that the crash is coming and you desperately need to rest. It's not a matter of *if* you'll crash at that point, just a matter of *when*.

You can do all this informally, of course, and I would venture to guess that the vast majority of bipolar people do just that. There are, however, many people out there who find great success in utilizing mood trackers. These can range anywhere from multi-part questionnaires you take every day to monitor all sorts of indicators, to simply keeping a journal and writing down how you felt each day. But the easier it is to tabulate in some fashion, the better. Maybe you write a couple of sentences each day and put a happy face, frowny face, or something similar to denote how you felt that day. If you want to get really fancy, I've even tried creating a Google Form and filling it out every day, which has the added benefits of being free and very customizable (not to mention making it easier to identify trends).

However you decide to do it (and there's a sample form in the appendix you can use or adapt as you see fit), the important thing is being able to track changes over time so you can see what, if any, patterns emerge. Maybe you tend to go manic every spring, which is not uncommon. Perhaps there's a predictable cycle you go through of mania and depression. Or maybe there are certain triggers that happen in your life that tend to push you one way or another. These things become much easier to track when you're keeping track of them, oddly enough. And whether you stick with it forever or just try it for a set amount of time, it will be helpful. I won't lie and say I still do it, but when I did, it definitely helped me pick up some patterns that were unique to me and my own bipolar experience, and I'm guessing it will do the same for you.

But what about depression? How does one know when that's coming on? Well, the good news is that it's typically a bit more obvious. That's not really because the symptoms are easier to identify, but rather because you're more inclined to believe them. When you're manic, and especially if you're not delusional or hallucinating, you want the mood to last forever. Mania feels great for a while. You're so productive and feel like you can do anything. Depression is the opposite. You can't wait for it to end. You might even, as many do, hasten to bring it to an end permanently through suicide. It's a dark place, and you won't want to stay there. But how do you know for sure that you're experiencing depression and not just in a bad mood? Again, the Mayo Clinic gives us symptoms, and they explain that you should be experiencing five or more of the following ones:

- *Depressed mood, such as feeling sad, empty, hopeless or tearful (in children and teens, depressed mood can appear as irritability)*
- *Marked loss of interest or feeling no pleasure in all — or almost all — activities*
- *Significant weight loss when not dieting, weight gain, or decrease or increase in appetite (in children, failure to gain weight as expected can be a sign of depression)*
- *Either insomnia or sleeping too much*
- *Either restlessness or slowed behavior*
- *Fatigue or loss of energy*
- *Feelings of worthlessness or excessive or inappropriate guilt*
- *Decreased ability to think or concentrate, or indecisiveness*
- *Thinking about, planning or attempting suicide[15]*

Depression can be tricky sometimes, because you can also get good at masking it. I've been in depressive episodes where all I wanted to do was go out every night and drink with friends. Maybe I was laughing and cracking jokes right along with everyone else, but inside I was just terrified of being alone. Other times, I've spent weeks sitting on the couch watching *Ink Master* episodes back-to-back-to-back, showering only occasionally and barely eating. I almost always get a ton of anxiety with my depression, as well, and find it difficult to imagine it ever being over. In fact, the one thing about being at both ends of the mood spectrum is I almost always find it impossible to remember (or even imagine) what it's like to be at the opposite end. That is to say, when I'm manic I can't imagine being depressed, and vice versa. And yet a shift always happens. Nothing lasts forever, and that's the silver lining.

That said, I was depressed for over a year one time because I was on the wrong meds (cough cough *Abilfy* cough cough), so if it's lasting that long, then you need to urge your doctor to switch up your

---

[15] Ibid.

medications and, if they won't, to get a new doctor. That's not a normal length of time to stay in one mood. But it's tricky for sure, because your depressive episode may last a few days, weeks, or even months, if you let it. And I say "let it" because there are absolutely things you can do to help reduce the negative effects of depression and start to reverse it. The problem is you never want to do them. But physical activity absolutely helps. I try to get myself to go to jiu-jitsu whenever I'm feeling depressed. I also try to cut out alcohol. This is a good idea whenever your mood isn't stable, but it's particularly important when you're depressed. Nothing makes a 12-gauge seem like a reasonable way to cope with your emotions quicker than alcohol. Unfortunately, you'll think it's helping you "deal with your emotions," but the reality is that alcohol is a depressant and that's the last thing you need when you're already depressed. Try weed instead. Or just learn to love non-alcoholic beers and clove cigarettes if you think you need to be sober.

*When times get tough emotionally, I turn to pottery. Or birdwatching. Or riding my motorcycle. Or bowling. Or listening to whale sounds. Just find something that works for you, dude.*

However you decide to do it, I strongly suggest trying to monitor your mood as best you can at all times, especially if you've never done it before. Of course, listening to your friends and loved ones is also important. My fiancée can tell I'm manic long before I typically can, because she isn't experiencing the mood changes herself and thus, she can be more impartial. She also has a vested interest in ensuring I *don't* become manic. But if you find yourself frequently getting into arguments with your special lady or man or nonbinary friend over whether or not you're manic, you're probably manic.

But of course, what does one do once they've admitted they have a problem? That looks different for everyone, but for me it's cutting out alcohol and adjusting my medications. In particular, I start taking an antipsychotic when I'm manic. I also start smoking more weed strains that help slow my brain down and make the racing thoughts take a break. Or, if I'm depressed, I find strains that help me deal with my anxiety and depression. I also force myself to take breaks when I'm manic and not hyper-focus on one thing all day, every day. When I'm depressed, sometimes self care is as simple as waking up while it's still morning and forcing myself to take a shower at least every other day.

Whatever it is that you end up doing, at least do something. Doing nothing about your symptoms and ignoring them is the fastest way to ruin your relationships, decimate your finances, lose your job, or end up at the hospital (or even in the ground, or with your ashes in a Folger's can, if you can only afford a modestly-priced receptacle). Don't just roll with it or roll over. I promise you, it won't work.

But can life actually be "good" while being someone who suffers from bipolar disorder? I'm here to tell you that it absolutely can, and will, if you learn how to abide through all of the strikes and gutters the illness throws your way by putting the right supports in place, which is what we'll talk about in the next chapter.

# Chapter 11

## The Dude Abides

### *What Supports to Put in Place*

So, is it possible for one to abide while being bipolar? The answer is yes, but you honestly can't do it (well) alone. The strikes and gutters are too extreme to handle without help. But all help is not equal. This book wouldn't be complete without an overview of some of the ways different people who are in your life, or who need to be in your life, can best support you in your journey.

Your first line of defense, of course, are your friends and family. Ideally, they will be honest with you, and they'll be willing to risk your wrath (when manic) or cold shoulder (when depressed) to tell you when you're not being completely honest with yourself or managing your condition well. This is much easier for others to do when you empower them to confront you when they see it going off the rails one way or another. At least in the United States, it's not seen as a good thing from a cultural standpoint to be seen as someone who meddles or "butts in" when their opinion isn't welcome, so people are often hesitant to do it. That's why it's important for your friends and family to know that you *want* them to intervene if they see you getting too high or too low. You will have to warn them that you may not listen, however, and having understanding friends who try and fail to get you to pay attention to the warning signs they're seeing is far superior to having friends who watch the warning signs fly by and do nothing (or worse – who enable your self-destructive behavior). You definitely should have other supports, but if you at least have supportive friends and family, then you have a fighting chance.

Another indispensable person you should have in your life is a good psychiatrist. Unfortunately, you're going to need this person for the rest of your life. No one likes an unmedicated bipolar person, and going off your meds is the greatest indicator of future problems. If you want to maintain a sense of balance and a semblance of predictability in your life, a good psych is essential. Now, I didn't always understand the difference between a psychiatrist and a therapist, but they're two very different (but important) types of support.

A psychiatrist is a doctor who can prescribe medications for you and help you find the right drug cocktail to keep you stable. They are similar to therapists in that they ask you about your life and how things are going, but they're doing it to try and assess where your mood is at and how to help you thrive from a medical standpoint while also doing their best to keep you from being admitted. They're not the ones you go to every week or month to talk through all your life's problems—that's what your therapist is for. More on that in a minute. What's important in a psychiatrist is that you trust them, and they listen to you. One thing reinforces the other, of course. There's nothing worse than a psychiatrist who doesn't listen or take your concerns into account when prescribing medications. They can easily end up doing more harm than good, just like a doctor who is dealing with your physical health. If you feel like your psych isn't listening or you don't trust them, it's time to have a frank conversation and/or move on to find another one. It's not easy to find a good psych, but it is worth it, for sure.

*Having friends and family who care for you when you can't is a huge benefit, and if you're lucky enough to have someone like my grandpa here, do your best to appreciate them.*

At this point it's probably worth noting that I'm putting these people in order of importance, at least as I see it. Friends and family members are crucial, as is a good psych. A good therapist is also important, especially if you've never been to one. I would argue that the longer you've lived with bipolar, the less essential they become. But if you've just recently been diagnosed, you should absolutely work with a therapist. I'd go for at least six months, going as often as every one to two weeks, at first. Possibly more often than that, if needed. A therapist is going to help you deal with everything that's not medication, although the good ones are also knowledgeable about medications as well. Try to find ones who specialize in working with people with bipolar, because every illness is unique, and experience does matter. Ideally, your therapist will help teach you about the disorder, generally, and help you better understand how it affects *you*, in particular. It's important to use them correctly, however, as you can't just expect to show up and have them "fix" you. You can make your sessions far more helpful to you and easier on them by preparing ahead of time. I have a note in my phone of things I want to talk with my therapist about, and it saves us both a lot of time. Some of them are problems that are unique to being bipolar while others are simply everyday problems that everyone deals with. Sometimes I don't know which kind of problem it is until I talk with my therapist, however.

You might be wondering if it's worth it to see a therapist, as they're not cheap and often they're not covered by insurance. I would argue that having someone you can be completely honest with about your fears and insecurities and who can be completely honest with you about what you need to work on is incredibly helpful. In my own mental health journey, I've been to many different therapists, and like psychiatrists, trust is essential. And I don't just mean you trust them to have your best interests at heart. I also mean that you trust who they are as a person. There are very few people outside of our friends and family who we give more power to in terms of knowing our deepest, darkest secrets, so if there's a mismatch between you and them in terms of values, it's going to color your treatment. I've left therapists because I thought their political or religious views were problematic. I've found that I don't really like working with male therapists either because I don't think they're as good at listening or identifying the relevant issues. I value having a different perspective and being challenged to think differently. Not all therapists are going to work for me, and the same therapist who I can't stand may be the ideal one for you (and vice versa.) The point is that it's a highly personal and idiosyncratic thing to find a therapist that works well for you, and finding one who syncs with your personality is far more important when it comes to therapy than it is when trying to find a good psych. I'll take a therapist I sync well with and whose worldview I share but who has to constantly consult the DSM-5 every session over one who graduated at the top of their class but is a straight white Republican guy. That's just never going to work for me. The important thing is to figure out what works for you, which is probably the biggest thread tying this whole 'derned book together.

Another thing that I have found to be incredibly helpful is belonging to a support group, especially a bipolar/mood disorder support group. I've belonged to one of these regularly for a while and I honestly struggled with whether or not to put it higher up on the list of "most important" types of relationships to have, because a good support group can be a great substitute for a therapist if you're not in a position financially to work with one. They can't really replicate what a psychiatrist does, but I would argue that they can be just as helpful in other ways. The benefit of a support group is that nearly everyone in the group knows what it's like to be in your shoes in one way or another, and that's rare to find. Having bipolar is something that you can explain to others, but recognizing racing thoughts in others is a very different thing from experiencing racing thoughts for yourself. Having an entire group of people who can hear what's happening in your life and instantly relate it to something they've experienced can be invaluable, particularly when you haven't gone through it yet. If nothing else, a support group makes you realize that you're not alone, and that other people are going through largely similar struggles and coming out of them OK. And, if you're having trouble finding one, why not join mine? Visit www.gemcitycircleofdudeists.org/bipolarsupport to learn more about when we meet.

Personally, I always find it equally as helpful to know, too, that there are bipolar people out there who are thriving and people out there who are in far worse places, as well. And, because you're all bipolar, you might be the unstable person one week and the one who has their shit together (relatively speaking) the next. Having that perspective, however, helps you realize that this, too, shall pass. The fact that absolutely nothing is permanent becomes incredibly empowering when you apply it to a mental health disorder. Being in a group like this helps you gain a perspective on the illness by recognizing that "it's all in your head," but not in the sense that this means it's easy to get over. I mean "it's all in your head" in the sense that it's a chemical imbalance that isn't permanent, and your life situation can be exactly the same from one week to the next while your perception of it is wildly different because it's dependent on your mood, not on your reality. I would argue that a support group is a useful tool for anyone suffering with bipolar, but if you find yourself lacking in other external sources of support (such as friends, family members, or mental health professionals), it's an indispensable tool that you can utilize to great effect.

And finally, I would be remiss if I didn't mention the most important relationship that you have to foster if you want to navigate life successfully while being bipolar: your relationship with yourself. You, at the end of the day, are the one constant in your life. Your thoughts and habits and ability to be disciplined about getting help are more important than any other relationship you have. Sometimes, it's all you have. That's why it's so important that you love yourself, are honest with yourself, and are always working to become a better version of yourself. That means working towards your dreams while operating firmly in reality. It means paying attention to your warning signs and taking corrective action whenever you're heading into trouble. It means planning ahead for the bad times so you can enjoy the good times. Most importantly, it means always striving to learn from your mistakes. Making a mistake isn't usually fatal. Repeatedly making the same mistakes over and over and over again, however, is the best recipe I know for losing jobs, financial security, relationships, and ultimately losing control over your life. Bipolar is a thief; don't let it take everything away that you hold dear.

But how, exactly, can you not only "get by" while living with bipolar disorder, but also thrive? That's what we'll talk about next in the final chapter.

# Chapter 12



## All The Dude Ever Wanted Was His Rug Back

*How to Abide in Life with Bipolar and Use Your Powers for Good*

Well, that about does her… wraps her all up. Well, that's most of it, at least. I guess if there's one thing I'd like you to leave this book with, it's hope, and the rationale for that hope is found in the fact that if you're bipolar (or know someone who is), then you get to see the world through a unique lens that less than 1% of the people in this universe get to experience (even if only vicariously through a bipolar loved one). Sometimes that lens makes this world into a beautiful, promising, and completely interconnected universe full of endless opportunities. Other times it makes you want to join the nearly 20% of bipolars who end up killing themselves. But say what you will about bipolar disorder, at least it's unique.

As I write this book, I'm somewhat manic… probably hypomanic. Because of that, I'm currently excited about the fact that so many threads of my different interests and beliefs and dreams are coming together, and it's an exciting time. I owe that vision becoming a reality equally to my fiancée and the "disease" that afflicts me. I owe it, in part, to my fiancée; for encouraging me and having the faith in and patience with me that is needed to allow me to pursue my passions. I owe it to the bipolar disorder for having many of those passions in the first place. In the words of the immortal John Prine, (whose old car and pinball machine now reside in the home of a friend of mine), "how lucky can one man get?"

And what are those dreams and visions, you might wonder? I thought you'd never ask.

You see, and this is just, like, my opinion, man, but I think that my life works best when three major ingredients are active for me, and those include: having something that grounds me, finding someone that complements me, and finding a way to make the world a slightly better place.

For me, the something that grounds me is Dudeism. I signed up for free by just typing in my email address and getting ordained, sending that ordination into the Secretary of State to get my license to marry, and then starting a TikTok channel where I talked about it a lot. Through that, I learned that there are so many more people out there who are Dudeists, and eventually I actually founded and incorporated a real (and legal... like, it has papers, man) 501c3 non-profit religious entity in Ohio. My goal now is to use it to create something I've always wanted to start: a Dudeist Retreat Center. It would have awesome workshops ranging from beekeeping to making maple syrup to home growing weed, and the campers (or "Achievers," perhaps) would stay in little tiny house shacks scattered throughout the property. Weed-infused s'mores and songs around the campfire would be the norm most evenings, and we'd definitely eat and drink and play well. If you will it, it is no dream, of course. Some fucking fascist said that, but it's true. If you'd like to know how close our goal is, you can always visit www.gemcitycircleofdudeists.org/donate to see how close we are to finally finding the venue we want.

*Wouldn't this old barn from that place I almost bought have been perfect? I thought I had finally found the venue I wanted, but it just wasn't to be. It will happen one day, though.*

As for the second pillar that I made up for this chapter, finding someone that complements you is pretty important for a lot of people, and that's possibly even truer for many bipolar ones. As for who, that's up to you. Maybe it's multiple people… polyamory has worked well for a lot of my bipolar friends and acquaintances because it allows several people to share the responsibility of helping the bipolar sufferer when they're going through it. Sometimes you might be lucky enough (like me) to find the one person who gets you and understands you and helps make sure you don't do stupid shit when your mood changes up one way or another. Or, and especially if you're not in a relationship, perhaps you need to become that other person for yourself. Put rules in place for yourself for what's going to help you abide when you become manic or depressed (or both) and stick to them.

Regardless of who they are, oftentimes the most important thing they can do for you is help you think through your decisions. Do you *really* need to pay twice of what it's worth for that empty plot of land or drop $6,000 on a travel agent certification course? Probably not. But having someone who you trust who can help you regulate those kinds of (potentially life-changing, and not in a good way) rash decisions can be a huge asset to you and can literally save you tons of wasted time and money. They can sometimes save your life. So find that special lady or guy or they/them friend, or become that person for yourself. Just be very cautious who you let in and make sure they understand the importance of keeping your trust. That's pretty key.

And, I mean, who *doesn't* want to make the world a better place? I'm not here to tell you how to do that, man. I've likely joined more political parties and religious denominations than most, and I was so confident every time I belonged to each of them that I wanted other people to join me. Hell, I fucking baptized some of my friends, man. Very un-dude. Maybe that's why I love Dudeism so much. I don't give a shit if you join or not, because I know it's a joke, like pretty much every religion that's out there. I'm not even so much trying to urge you to do anything, really. What I would advise, however, is being humble about whatever you do. That doesn't mean letting aggressions stand, however, especially when someone clearly steps over the line. This isn't 'Nam, man, there are rules. But you know, like, maybe just focus on being yourself, whoever that is (and will become). I'd also recommend listening to other bipolar people out there, and I've included an appendix page full of bipolar TikTok creators and accounts that I think you should check out, both for advice and for inspiration.

Now, of course, this book bills itself as being able to help you not just get by, but abide. I would argue that when you're properly medicated and have figured out your relationships and how to get the support you need, you can truly thrive as a bipolar person because you see the world through a unique lens. In the words of the Dudely Saint, Kurt Vonnegut, Jr., in his book *Timequake*, "Many people need desperately to receive this message: 'I feel and think much as you do, care about many of the things you care about, although most people do not care about them. You are not alone.'" You see the world differently, and there's nothing wrong with that. In fact, there's a lot that's great about it. You see connections that other people miss. You see what's possible when others see nothing at all.

Allow me to brag for just a moment (for illustrative purposes only, of course). I started an exchange program with no money and ended up turning it into a $120,000 US Department of State grant that (now annually) brings over 18 students and three teachers from Bosnia and Herzegovina to Dayton, OH, the home of the Dayton Peace Accords, which ended the war in Bosnia back in the 1990s. I've helped design numerous cross-curricular, project-based learning units as a teacher, as well, because I was able to see how different subjects and topics complemented and synced well with one another. If I haven't made it clear by now, I want you to know that I firmly believe that *you also* possess some unique skills and ways of thinking as a bipolar person that others simply don't have, so don't let anyone tell you that you don't deserve a seat at the table (regardless of where that table is) because of your disorder. If anything, they need people like you more than you need them.

Now that we're coming to the end of this book, I'll recommend some others for you to put on your bipolar reading list. One would be Kay Redfield Jamison's *Touched With Fire*, a book examining the link between bipolar disorder and creativity. It's not just, like, my opinion that bipolar people tend to be more creative. It's science, man. And Dr. Jamison is a psychologist who also suffers from bipolar disorder, so she should know. Her other books are good, too, including her must-read memoir, *An Unquiet Mind*, which I would consider to be a "classic" in the bipolar disorder book realm.

Another bipolar doctor who wrote a book that I really love (and found incredibly helpful) happens to be the son of my all-time favorite author, who (if you haven't already figured out by now) is Kurt Vonnegut. His son, Mark Vonnegut, is also an author, and my favorite book of his is *Just Like Someone Without Mental Illness Only More So*. It's another memoir that I can't recommend enough and that will give you a really good sense of what living with bipolar disorder is really like.

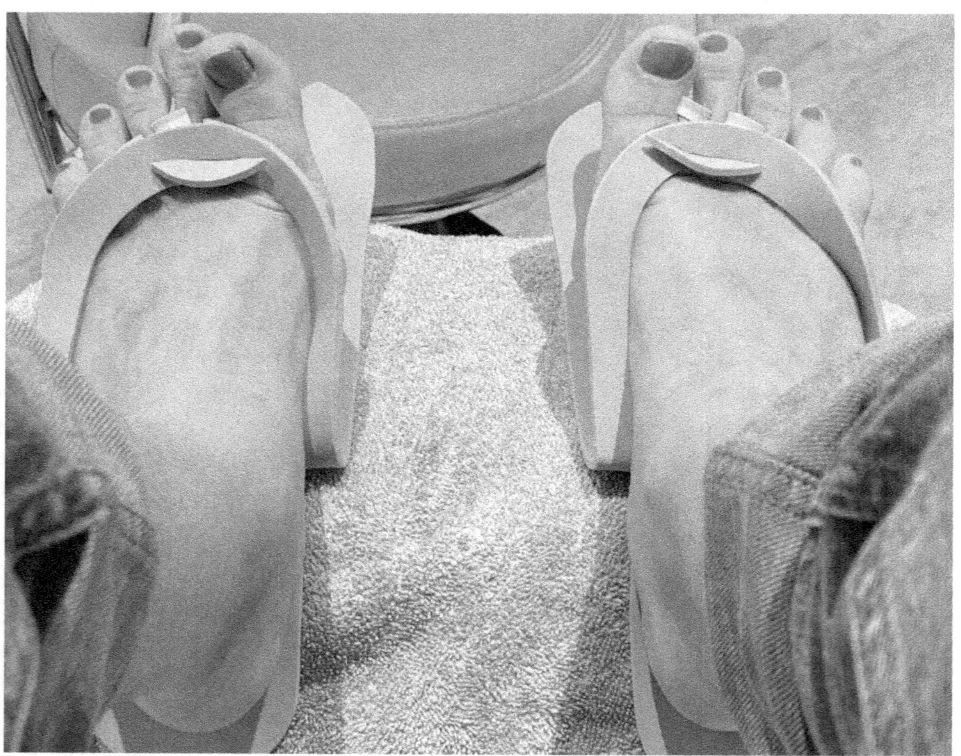

*I like to channel Bunny when I get a pedicure and go with the neon green toenails, personally.*

A (likely fake) quote (supposedly from) Lao Tzu goes something like, "the snow goose need not bathe to make itself white. Neither need you do anything but be yourself." And I don't know about you, but I take comfort in that. And, I mean, for that matter, I'll even admit that Jesus and Buddha and Mohammed all said some cool shit sometimes. But so did Coi Leray, bell hooks, Anthony Bourdain, Kurt Vonnegut, James Baldwin, and fellow Daytonian Erma Bombeck. You've said some cool shit, too, I'm sure. So just be yourself (and take care of yourself, too). That, and become a semi-ironic leftist, just like Jeffrey. But I'll save that book for another day. For now, just abide, dudes.

8 5

# Acknowledgements

Living with bipolar disorder isn't easy, and sometimes it takes a village to help someone who suffers from it. I am no exception in this regard, and there are too many people to thank individually. I would like to thank all the friends who have stuck with me over the years. I've given most (if not all) of them reasons not to, but the real ones haven't left me, and I can't thank them enough for that. I'd also like to thank my family. Sure, I have my differences with a lot of them, but whenever I've struggled, they nearly always step up and help out.

I'd also like to thank the community of people who encourage me on TikTok. It might sound strange, but in many ways they're closer friends than ones I know in "real life," and as I've shared my struggles with them over the years, they have stuck with me through the highs and lows and made me feel like I have something to contribute to the bipolar disorder discussion, and I can't thank them enough for that. I would like to thank my friend Mary Theadoor (@marynown on TikTok) in particular for designing the cover art for the book, which is one thing I didn't feel like I could do myself. I would like to thank my brother, Patrick, and fiancée, Jay, for editing this book for me. Thanks to them I have been able to achieve my goal of publishing it without spending a dime, and that (as a bipolar person especially) is somewhat of a miracle.

I also want to give a special thanks to my special lady friend/fiancée, Jay, who chose to spend her life with me even after knowing just how bad things can get when the mania or depression are at their worst. There's no one else who gets me like she does or makes me happier in this world, and I'm so glad I get to spend the rest of my life with her.

# Where to Find Me

TikTok: @gemcitydudeistpriest

Instagram: @gemcitydudeistpriest

Facebook: @gemcitydudeistpriest

YouTube: @gemcitydudeistpriest

Web: www.gemcitydudeistpriest.com

Email: gemcitydudeistpriest@gmail.com

Podcasts: Killing Time With Arch & The Discover Dayton
Podcast

The Gem City Circle of Dudeists:
www.gemcitycircleofdudeists.org

Bipolar Support Group:
www.gemcitycircleofdudeists.org/bipolarsupport

Find other formats of this book at:
www.gemcitydudeistpriest.com/bipolardudebook

Find my Substack at:
www.gemcitydudeistpriest.substack.com

# Appendix

This appendix includes all of the tools I talked about in the book, and it is my hope that you will find them helpful in managing your own bipolar disorder (or helping a loved one do so).

The bipolar mood scale is a good tool for helping you and/or your loved ones identify what state of mood you're currently in, which is incredibly important for figuring out how to best manage your symptoms and care.

The mania contract is a very useful tool as well for helping make it easier for you to agree to a treatment plan when you don't believe you need to seek help.

Similarly, the suicide safety plan can literally be a lifesaver in helping you as you try and claw your way out of a deep depression.

The mood tracker is also very helpful, especially if you're newly diagnosed or haven't used one before. It can help reveal trends or identify potential stressors that you might not otherwise see as causal when you're ramping up or going down in mood.

Finally, it's always helpful seeing other people who are going through the same things you are in life, so I've included a list of people I follow on TikTok who I think do a good job of giving advice or inspiration to people with bipolar. I hope these tools help you as much as they've helped me, if not more.

*To download digital versions all of the materials in this appendix for free, visit www.gemcitydudeistpriest.com/bipolardudeguide and give me your email!*

| | | |
|---|---|---|
| **Mania** | **10** | Crazy spending habits, completely delusional, totally irrational behavior, and hallucinations. |
| | **9** | No longer able to differentiate between reality and delusions, paranoia, impulsive and/or spiteful behavior, not sleeping. |
| **Hypomania** | **8** | Delusions of grandeur, rapid speech/thoughts, working inefficiently on multiple projects at once. |
| | **7** | Highly productive, indulgent behavior (calling/texting/smoking/caffeine/drugs), overly friendly and chatty. |
| **Balanced Mood** | **6** | High self-esteem, good outlook on life, highly engaging in social situations, rational decision-making, and productive. |
| | **5** | Balanced mood with no manic or depressive tendencies. Symptoms of bipolar mood swings are absent. |
| | **4** | Slightly withdrawn, slight difficulty concentrating, more easily agitated than usual. |
| **Mild/Moderate Depression** | **3** | Anxious and difficult to focus due to poor memory. Still capable of doing most usual tasks/routines. |
| | **2** | Sluggish thoughts, little to no desire to eat, sleeping too much or too little, difficulty accomplishing most things. |
| **Severe Depression** | **1** | Hopeless in life outlook, strong feelings of guilt, suicidal thoughts, extreme difficulty even with simple tasks. |
| | **0** | Constant thoughts of suicide, feelings of being trapped or unable to move, numbness, and no hope for the future. |

# Mania Contract for Person with Bipolar and Family Members, Friends, or Caregivers

## Intro

This contract between ____________________________ (bipolar sufferer) and ____________________________ (caregiver) was entered into on ____/____/______ to help ensure that the person suffering from bipolar gets the help they need when they need it most.

## Bipolar sufferer info

Name:____________________________________
DOB:____/____/_____
Psychiatrist: ____________________________ Phone: ____________________________ Address: ____________________________
Therapist: ____________________________ Phone: ____________________________ Address: ____________________________
Trusted friend (to help if caretaker cannot): ____________________________ Phone: ____________________________

## Agreed upon symptoms of hypomania

- Less sleep/dramatic sleep schedule changes
- Increased calling/texting family and friends
- Being irritated when others disagree/higher level of irritation in general
- Increase in amount of time spent working on hobbies/new interests
- Small paranoias
- Feeling "really good" (more energy, more productive than usual), including lots of goal-oriented behaviors
- More talkative
- Increased sex drive
- _______________________________________
- _______________________________________
- _______________________________________
- _______________________________________
- _______________________________________

# Agreed upon symptoms of mania

- Seeing connections everywhere
- Slipping into "7<sup>th</sup> gear" thinking/racing thoughts
- Sudden changes in feelings towards loved ones
- Delusions of grandeur
- Paranoia/conspiratorial thinking
- Delusions/hallucinations/psychosis
- _______________________________________________
- _______________________________________________
- _______________________________________________
- _______________________________________________
- _______________________________________________

## Agreements

- __________ will be in bed by 1AM and get 6+ hours of sleep per night at a minimum.
- __________ will take medications as prescribed by psych for when they slip into hypomania or mania.
- __________ will wait for a calm time to tell __________ they're manic and need to begin to make changes.
- __________ will not make any investment decisions alone.
- __________ will schedule an appointment with or contact their therapist and then, if they deem necessary, their psychiatrist.

***By signing below both parties agree to the hypomania and mania symptoms and agreements spelled out in this document.***

## Signatures

Name: _________________ Signed: _________________ Date: __/__/__

Name: _________________ Signed: _________________ Date: __/__/__

# Suicide Safety Plan for Depression

**Early warning signs of depression for me include:**
- Feelings of anxiety, panic, or helplessness and lack of interest in activities I normally enjoy.
- _______________________________________________
- _______________________________________________

**Risk reduction steps I will take when feeling depressed or suicidal:**
- Cut out alcohol and take any medications my doctor prescribes for me when I am anxious and depressed.
- Give my weapons and blades to my friend, _______________.
- _______________________________________________

**Coping methods I will employ when depressed or suicidal:**
- I will do some type of physical activity each day, such as yoga, jiu-jitsu, riding my bike, or just walking around the block.
- I will talk with my therapist at least once per week and journal.
- _______________________________________________
- _______________________________________________

**Mantras I will meditate on during my depression:**
- I have been through this before, and I will make it through this time.
- _______________________________________________
- _______________________________________________

**What my friends and family members can do to help me:**
- Hang out with me where I'm at, whether that be going to events or hanging out at home.
- Inviting me to dinner while being conscious of my desire to cut out alcohol during my period of depression.
- _______________________________________________

**When extremely depressed and/or suicidal, I'll call:**
- Friend/loved one: _______ / ____-_____  2nd: _______ / ____-_____
- Psychiatrist: _______ / ____-_____  Therapist: _______ / ____-_____
- Hospital: _______ / ____-_____  Pysch Hospital: _______ / ____-_____
- Emergency Suicide Hotline/SMS: 988 (US)

**Directions:** Use the mood tracker below by placing an "X" for where your mood was (primarily) that day, writing in the number of hours you slept placing an "X" next to any of the things that took place that day.

| | Mood rating | Day 1 | Day 2 | Day 3 | Day 4 | Day 5 | Day 6 | Day 7 |
|---|---|---|---|---|---|---|---|---|
| **High mood (6-10)** | 10 | | | | | | | |
| | 9 | | | | | | | |
| | 8 | | | | | | | |
| | 7 | | | | | | | |
| | 6 | | | | | | | |
| **Balanced mood (5)** | 5 | | | | | | | |
| **Low mood (0-4)** | 4 | | | | | | | |
| | 3 | | | | | | | |
| | 2 | | | | | | | |
| | 1 | | | | | | | |
| | 0 | | | | | | | |
| **Hours slept last night:** | | | | | | | | |
| **Anxiety?** | | | | | | | | |
| **Irritability?** | | | | | | | | |
| **Taken meds?** | | | | | | | | |
| **Physical exercise?** | | | | | | | | |
| **Unusual stressors?** | | | | | | | | |

| Day 1 Notes | Day 2 Notes | Day 3 Notes | Day 4 Notes | Day 5 Notes | Day 6 Notes | Day 7 Notes |
|---|---|---|---|---|---|---|
| | | | | | | |

# Bipolar Disorder TikTok Accounts Worth Following

@angelfromthebloc

@beccharlwood

@bipolarbetch

@bipolarbetty

@bipolargayguy

@catherinezetajones

@ddlovato

@freighttrainthrowsdiscs

@gemcitydudeistpriest (me)

@mariahcarey

@randallinaustin

@raisingcrazy

@selenagomez

@taylortomlinsoncomedy

@tevynharmon

@thebpspouse

@therealbruss

@this.is.bipolar